IRAQI AIR POWER REBORN, The Iraqi air arms since

Arnaud Delalande

IRAQI AIR POWER REBORN

The Iraqi air arms since 2004

Arnaud Delalande

HARPIA
PUBLISHING +

Consulting and inspiration by Kerstin Berger
Artworks by Tom Cooper
Map by James Lawrence
Editorial by Thomas Newdick
Layout by Norbert Novak, www.media-n.at, Vienna

Printed at Grasl FairPrint, Austria

Harpia Publishing, L.L.C. is a member of

ISBN 978-0-9854554-7-7

Contents

Acknowledgements 7

Abbreviations 8

Chapter 1: The former Iraqi Air Force 11

Chapter 2: Aircraft of the 'new' Iraqi Air Force 19
    Fighter and attack aircraft 19
    Reconnaissance aircraft 26
    Transport aircraft 30
    Training aircraft 33

Chapter 3: Aircraft of Iraqi Army Aviation 37
    Attack aircraft 37
    Armed reconnaissance aircraft 40
    Transport and special operations aircraft 44
    Unmanned aerial vehicles 52
    Training aircraft 53

Chapter 4: Future aircraft 57

Chapter 5: IQAF and IAA at war 59

Appendix I: Orders of battle 71
            Map of Iraq 73

Appendix II: Attrition 75

Bibliography 77

Acknowledgements

The author wishes to express his particular gratitude to all those individuals who contributed to this book. Foremost among these are several Iraqi Air Force and Army Aviation pilots active on the Iraqi Air Force Facebook page. Some of them granted interviews only on the condition of anonymity. Several Iraqi military and civilian individuals also provided many photographs and extensive aid in translation; the author wishes to express special thanks to them. Sadly, the author does not feel at liberty to name any such individual in public and in several cases will only be able to forward his thanks privately.

Other assistance was provided by a number of researchers elsewhere, all of whom kindly helped during the preparation of this book, in particular: Hamza Abbas, Mohamad Bahia, Tom Cooper, Marco Dijkshoorn, Babak Khabazan, and Babak Taghvaee. All of them provided extensive aid in the form of related research and ultimately made this book possible.

Arnaud Delalande, March 2016

Abbreviations

ALAT	Aviation de Légère de l'Armée de Terre (French Army Light Aviation)
AMRAAM	Advanced Medium-Range Air-to-Air Missile
AB	Air Base
AFB	Air Force Base (used for US Air Force bases)
ANG	Air National Guard (US)
ANGB	Air National Guard Base (US)
Brig Gen	brigadier general (military commissioned officer rank)
Capt	captain (military commissioned officer rank)
CAS	close air support
CBW	Composite Bomber Wing
c/n	construction number
CO	commanding officer
COB	Contingency Operating Base
COIN	counter-insurgency
Col	colonel (military commissioned officer rank)
Col Gen	colonel-general (top military commissioned officer rank)
DoD	Department of Defense (US)
FS	Fighter Squadron
FTS	Flying Training School
FS	Fighter Wing
Gen	general (military commissioned officer rank)
HQ	headquarters
IAA	Iraqi Army Aviation
IAP	international airport
IFTS	Iraqi Flight Training School
IQAF	Iraqi Air Force (used from 2003, previously IrAF)
IrAAC	Iraqi Army Aviation Corps
IrAF	Iraqi Air Force (used from 1958 until 2003, thereafter IQAF)
IRGCASF	Islamic Revolutionary Guards Corps Air and Space Force
IRIAF	Islamic Republic of Iran Air Force
IS	Islamic State
ISR	intelligence, surveillance and reconnaissance
KIA	killed in action
1st Lt	first lieutenant (military commissioned officer rank)
2nd Lt	second lieutenant (lowest military commissioned officer rank)
Lt	lieutenant (military commissioned officer rank)
Lt Col	lieutenant colonel (military commissioned officer rank)
Maj	major (military commissioned officer rank)
Maj Gen	major general (military commissioned officer rank)
MANPADS	man-portable air defence system(s) – light surface-to-air missile system that can be carried and deployed in combat by a single soldier
MoD	Ministry of Defense (Iraq)
NAS	Naval Air Station
NFZ	'no-fly' zone
ORBAT	order of battle

RAF	Royal Air Force (of the United Kingdom)
RIrAF	Royal Iraqi Air Force, 1931 to 1958
RJAF	Royal Jordanian Air Force
SA-7 Grail	ASCC codename for 9K32 Strela-2, Soviet MANPADS
SA-24 Grinch	ASCC codename for 9K338 Igla-S, Russian MANPADS
SAM	surface-to-air missile
SyAAF	Syrian Arab Air Force
UAE	United Arab Emirates
UAEAF	United Arab Emirates Air Force
UAV	unmanned aerial vehicle
UK	United Kingdom
UN	United Nations
US	United States
USAF	United States Air Force
USD	United States Dollar
USSR	Union of Soviet Socialist Republics (or Soviet Union)
VBIED	vehicle-borne improvised explosive device
WIA	wounded in action

THE FORMER IRAQI AIR FORCE

The Royal Iraqi Air Force (RIrAF) was created on 22 April 1931 and was initially based at Washash Airport near Baghdad. At the time, Iraq was under a mandate of the League of Nations (since 1920) and was administered by the United Kingdom. At the time of its conception, the RIrAF was composed of five pilots and 32 aircraft technicians. Students underwent training at RAF College Cranwell in England. During the first years after its creation, the RIrAF was equipped with British aircraft including the Hawker Fury and Hawker Audax. After independence, and the foundation of the Kingdom of Iraq in 1932, the RIrAF began to acquire Italian aircraft, including Breda Ba.65 ground-attack aircraft and Savoia-Marchetti S.M.79 Sparviero medium bombers. However, in the years following Iraqi independence, the RIrAF remained heavily dependent upon the supervision and advice of the British Royal Air Force. Although the Iraqi government allocated most of its defence spending to the Army, between 1936 and 1937 the number of pilots qualified to fly the 55 available aircraft increased from 36 to 127. In 1934, the RIrAF was engaged in combat for the first time. Under the orders of Brig Gen Bakr Sidqi, the RIrAF was employed against tribal revolts in Diwaniya and Rumaytha in the south of Iraq and in the process suffered its first combat loss.

The RIrAF was engaged in combat for a second time during the short but bitter Anglo-Iraqi War of May 1941 (also known as the Rashid Ali Uprising). Encouraged by Nazi Germany, a considerable proportion of the Iraqi military staged a coup against the pro-British government in Baghdad and moved against the major British military bases in Habbaniyah and Basra. At the time, the RIrAF was organised into four operational squadrons and the Flying Training School (FTS) located at al-Rashid near Baghdad (the former RAF Hinaidi), plus two operational squadrons based at Mosul. These operated a miscellany of Ba.65 and Douglas Model 8A light bombers, de Havilland Dragon and Dragonfly general-purpose biplanes, de Havilland Tiger Moth biplane trainers, Gloster Gladiator biplane fighters, Hawker Nisr (Iraqi Audax) army cooperation aircraft, S.M.79 medium bombers, and Vickers Vincent biplane light bombers.

Although it bombed RAF Habbaniyah several times, the RIrAF failed to provide top cover for Iraqi Army forces besieging the British base. Furthermore, like the Iraqi ground forces, the RIrAF suffered terribly under RAF air strikes on al-Rashid and Baquba airfields. Indeed, the British destroyed nearly 70 and damaged up to 30 aircraft on the ground between 4 and 6 May. The Iraqi mutineers thus failed to buy time for Germany to bring arms and aircraft into the country, as Berlin had promised. As a consequence, by the time German forces did appear – arriving via Vichy-controlled Syria, in mid-May 1941 – the morale of the Iraqi military was shattered, and the RIrAF was destroyed as a fighting force.

The very first aircraft of the Royal Iraqi Air Force: a de Havilland D.H.60 Moth with the serial number 1, seen in 1931.
(Tom Cooper Collection)

In 1948 the Avro Ansons of Nos 1 and 7 Squadrons became the first Iraqi aircraft to see involvement in combat with Israel.
(Pit Weinert Collection)

A mixed formation of IrAF Hunter F.Mk 6s and UARAF MiG-17s in 1958.
(David Nicolle Collection)

1948 Arab-Israeli War

The Arab-Israeli conflict of 1948 came at a time in which the RIrAF was still recovering from its destruction by the British and in the midst of transition from older aircraft to more advanced equipment such as the Hawker Fury monoplane fighter. Despite this, the RIrAF played a small role in the first war against Israel. Two squadrons equipped with Avro Anson bomber-trainers were dispatched to Jordan and Syria, from where they flew a number of combat sorties. During the late summer of 1948, Ansons were progressively replaced by brand-new Fury fighters, 55 of which were eventually purchased from the UK. Assigned to Nos 7 and 9 Squadrons, RIrAF, but hampered by a lack of ammunition and spares, the Furies flew a limited number of combat sorties from Damascus, before at least four were donated to Egypt in late 1948. Their pilots claimed the destruction of an Israeli Air Force Boeing B-17 Flying Fortress bomber on the ground and the sinking of a merchant vessel bringing supplies to the port of Haifa.

The jet age

In 1953 the RIrAF began purchasing its first jet fighters, in the form of 12 de Havilland Vampire FB.Mk 52s, six Vampire T.Mk 55 trainers, and 19 Venom FB.Mk 1 and FB.Mk 50 fighter-bombers. As soon as two units had become operational on these types, the RIrAF pushed for the acquisition of more modern jets, and demanded Hawker Hunters from the UK and North American F-86 Sabres from the US, together with either British- or US-manufactured Canberra bombers. After lengthy negotiations, the US agreed to sponsor the purchase of 16 Hunters from the UK, as well as deliver 24 F-86Fs and 12 F-86Ds from US Air Force stocks to Iraq. While 15 Hunters (one crashed during training in the UK) entered service in early 1958, only five Sabres were delivered before the 14 Tammuz (14 July) Revolution toppled the monarchy and the young King of Iraq. The Sabres thus never entered service: they were stored within a hangar at al-Rashid airfield before being returned to the US in 1963.

The 1958 coup put an end to cooperation with Western nations, in particular the UK, and Baghdad instead established relationships with the Soviet Union. As a result of the coup the RIrAF became the Iraqi Air Force (IrAF), and it started to receive 14 Mikoyan-Gurevich MiG-17F (in 1958), 50 MiG-19 (1962) and 60 MiG-21F-13 fighters (1962) from the USSR, followed by 12 Ilyushin Il-28 bombers.

The following decade saw numerous coup attempts that resulted in changes, restructuring and large-scale purges within the IrAF. A new government installed after the coup of February 1963 re-established relations with the UK and for a three-year period the purchase of Soviet fighters and bombers came to an end. Meanwhile, more Hunters were ordered. A total of 16 Hunter F.Mk 6s, 22 Hunter F.Mk 59s, 18 Hunter F.Mk 59As, four Hunter F.Mk 59Bs, between three and five Hunter T.Mk 69A two-seaters, and several Hunter FR.Mk 10s were delivered to the IrAF. Following the death of Iraqi President Abdul Salam Arif, in the crash of an IrAF Mil Mi-4 helicopter on 13 April 1966, and his replacement by his brother, Abdul Rahman, Iraq purchased a batch of MiG-21FL fighters from the Soviet Union. On 16 August 1966, an Iraqi pilot, Munir Redfa, was forced to defect to Israel with his MiG-21F-13 during an operation undertaken by the Israeli Mossad (Operation Diamond).

1967 Arab-Israeli War

The new MiG-21FLs arrived in time for the June 1967 War. Indeed, the first examples from a follow-on batch of MiG-21PFMs ordered from the USSR began to arrive in May 1967. Most of the MiG-21FLs from No. 17 Squadron were re-deployed to H-3 airfield together with Hunters from Nos 6 and 29 Squadrons, in preparation for their further deployment to Mafraq airfield, in Jordan, planned for 5 June 1967. MiG-21FLs flew around 30 combat air patrols from H-3 on 5 and 6 June, and participated in at least two air combats with Israeli aircraft. In contrast, most of Iraq's MiG-21F-13s were undergoing overhaul in the USSR during the war.

On 5 June 1967, five Hunters of No. 6 Squadron carried out air strikes against Petah Tikva airfield, claiming the destruction of seven Israeli Nord Noratlas and Douglas Dakota transports on the ground, while three other Hunters attacked Lod international airport (IAP). In retaliation, four Israeli Sud Aviation Vautours escorted by two Dassault Mirage IIIs raided H-3, destroying three MiG-21s, one Hunter, one Antonov An-12 and a Dove in the course of the afternoon. The day after, six Hunters attacked Israeli armour near Jenin. By the time the Hunters recovered to H-3, Israeli aircraft had arrived over the airfield while another two Hunters were taking off. One Hunter crashed, killing its pilot, while the other engaged in fruitless combat against a Vautour and a Mirage. During the same morning, four Tupolev Tu-16 bombers launched attacks against Israel. Two of them reached Israeli airspace, however, they missed Ramat David airfield and instead bombed the town of Netanya. One was shot down by a combination of Israeli Mirages and ground fire while egressing at low altitude.

On 7 June, following the relocation of IrAF fighters to Habbaniyah and the reinforcement of No. 6 Squadron by around a dozen Jordanian and one Pakistani pilot, the Hunters engaged in dogfights with Vautours and Mirages that were once again attacking H-3. One Hunter, two Vautours and two Mirages were shot down in air combat.

Another coup took place on 17 July 1968, this time conducted by military units including elements of the IrAF and the Ba'ath Party. In the following years, Iraq signed new treaties with the USSR covering the purchase of modern jet fighters including Sukhoi Su-7s and MiG-21s. The IrAF received its first 18 Su-7BMKs in 1968, but Iraq was less than satisfied with the aircraft supplied by the Soviets, and instead turned to France in an effort to acquire Mirage 5s and SEPECAT Jaguars.

Between 1961 and 1984, Iraq purchased over 200 MiG-21s of nearly a dozen different variants. This photograph shows MiG-21bis serial number 21185 in the 1990s.
(Pit Weinert Collection)

1973 Arab-Israeli War

In April 1973, 24 Hunter F.Mk 59s from Nos 6 and 29 Squadrons were deployed to Egypt for joint exercises with the Egyptian Air Force. The aircraft remained in Egypt to fight in the 1973 Arab-Israeli War. On 7 October 1973 the IrAF began deploying no fewer than six of its units to Syria, including Su-7BMKs from Nos 1, 5 and 8 Squadrons, MiG-21s from Nos 9 and 11 Squadrons, and MiG-17s from No. 7 Squadron. Moreover, all available transport aircraft and helicopters were involved in supporting this deployment and the deployment of two Iraqi Army divisions to the front lines on the Golan Heights. Over the following two weeks, IrAF units saw considerable participation in the fighting against Israel, flying with generally effective results in around 750 combat sorties or 862 hours in combat (including 121 over the Egyptian front and 394 over

Operated by two squadrons, Hawker Hunters represented the backbone of the IrAF fighter-bomber fleet during the 1960s and early 1970s.
(David Nicolle Collection)

the Syrian). Most of these combat sorties consisted of combat air patrols flown by MiG-21s and MiG-17s, resulting in dozens of air combats with Israeli fighters. Iraqi pilots claimed 22 aerial victories, and three pilots were officially credited with five confirmed 'kills'. Iraqi attrition was heavy too, and included the loss of 15 Su-7BMKs, eight Hunters, five MiG-21s, and two MiG-17s. Two Iraqi pilots became prisoners of war in Israel, while 12 were killed in action.

Involvement in the October 1973 War with Israel represented a critical experience for the IrAF, heavily influencing its further development and procurement, as well as shaping doctrine and tactics for the next decade.

Fighting the Kurds and border incidents with Iran

Beginning in 1962 and continuing into the early 1970s, the IrAF had been involved in a continuous war against fierce Kurdish uprisings in the north of the country. These not only provided plenty of combat experience for the pilots involved, but also had a significant influence upon Baghdad's combat aircraft procurement policy at the time. The situation culminated in late 1974, when the Shah of Iran deployed units of the regular Imperial Iranian Army, supported by heavy artillery and modern surface-to-air missiles (SAMs), on the side of the Kurdish insurgents. In just a few weeks the Iranian SAMs shot down up 15 Iraqi combat aircraft, thereby denying freedom of action to the IrAF. The only aircraft to continue operations against the Kurds were the brand-new Tu-22 bombers, 16 of which had been delivered shortly before the October 1973 War. Operating at supersonic speeds and high altitude, and deploying massive FAB-1500 and FAB-3000 bombs from stand-off distances, these delivered a number of blows against the insurgents.

Iraqi Air Force Tupolev Tu-22 bombers saw their first combat during operations against Kurdish insurgents in northern Iraq, in 1974–75.
(Tom Cooper Collection)

Nevertheless, the experience of the Iranian SAMs and the major demonstrations of power by the Imperial Iranian Air Force along the Shatt al-Arab made a significant impression upon Baghdad. In 1975 the government accepted an Algerian-negotiated peace treaty with Tehran, according to which both sides agreed to the status quo regarding the mutual border and ceased supporting oppositional forces. Iranian support for the Iraqi Kurds came to an end and no further incidents took place until 1980.

Iran–Iraq War

Mirage F.1EQ 4010 still in France prior to its delivery to Iraq in April 1981.
(Tom Cooper Collection)

Immediately prior to the Iraqi invasion of Iran in autumn 1980, the IrAF inventory included around 340 aircraft. In late September 1980 the delivery of 16 Mirage F.1EQs from France and another 240 aircraft and helicopters from the Soviet Union was stopped, only to resume a few months later. Therefore, in the first months of the war the IrAF had to fight with outdated equipment including Su-20s for ground attack, MiG-21s for interception and MiG-23s for interception and ground attack.

On 22 September Iraq launched 220 air strikes against 10 Iranian air bases, airports, and army bases. Intended to crater runways and thus 'ground' the Islamic Republic of Iran Air Force (IRIAF) for the first 48 hours of the war, the attack did not have the desired impact. On the contrary, the IRIAF hit back in force the same afternoon, and in even greater force on the morning of 23 September, when it launched a massive,

140-aircraft strike against Iraqi air bases. The IrAF was thus forced on to the defensive from the start of the war. The situation remained the same for the next four months, during which Iraqi MiG-21s and MiG-23s were primarily busy flying combat air patrols with the aim of intercepting low-flying IRIAF McDonnell Douglas F-4 Phantom IIs and Northrop F-5 Tiger IIs that were striking targets across Iraq. Although around two dozen Iranian fighter-bombers were shot down by MiGs and SAMs, most of Iraq's oil industry was badly damaged and had been put out of operation by the end of the year.

Beginning in late 1981, the IrAF pressed into service an entirely new generation of combat aircraft, including Mirage F.1s, MiG-25s, and new variants of the Su-22. These aircraft had been provided together with an assortment of advanced French and Soviet-made weapons, and were to bear the brunt of the fighting against Iran for the next seven years.

In October 1982 the French government took the decision to 'lease' to Iraq five Dassault Super Étendards pending delivery of Mirage F.1EQ5s that were capable of launching AM.39 Exocet anti-ship missiles. The Super Étendards were deployed in an effort to curb exports of Iranian crude from Khark Island, in turn sparking the so-called 'Tanker War', in 1984. On 27 March that year they sank the South Korean tanker *Heyang Ilho* and damaged the Greek tanker *Filikon L*. Iranian pilots claimed several Super Étendards shot down, but only one failed to return to France: it was shot down in 1984 by an IRIAF Grumman F-14A Tomcat.

In 1984, Maj Gen Sha'ban took over command of the IrAF. He initiated a number of major reforms, aimed at transforming the Air Force into a branch that would have a decisive impact on the outcome of war against Iran. One of Sha'ban's first decisions was to order the IrAF to launch raids against Iranian industry and economic targets – foremost the oil-exporting terminal on Khark Island and shipping involved in the export of Iranian crude.

The Exocet missiles launched from Super Étendards, Mirage F.1EQ5s and Aérospatiale Super Frelon helicopters hit a large number of foreign trade vessels (in total, over 500 vessels were hit by Iraqi and Iranian forces during the course of the war). On 17 May 1987, two Exocet missiles launched by a modified Dassault Falcon 50 hit the American frigate USS *Stark*, crippling the ship and killing 37 sailors. On 20 July 1988, Iran accepted Resolution 598, demonstrating its willingness to accept a ceasefire.

Invasion of Kuwait and the Gulf War

By summer 1990 the IrAF maintained a force of over 480 combat aircraft and 230 helicopters. On 2 August, Iraqi forces invaded Kuwait. Initially, the Iraqi Army deployed its Mi-25 combat helicopters as well as its Mi-8/17 and Bell 412 helicopters to transport commandos into Kuwait City. In support of the invasion the IrAF deployed two squadrons of MiG-23s, one of Mirage F.1s, two of Su-22s and one of Su-25s. Their targets were the two main Kuwaiti air bases, as well as other objectives in the capital. The IrAF lost two fighter-bombers during the invasion of Kuwait, a MiG-23BN and a Su-22, both shot down by ground fire. Kuwaiti McDonnell Douglas A-4KU Skyhawks and Mirage F.1CKs claimed 15 Iraqi helicopters shot down, but according to Iraq, only three were lost: a Bell 412ST, a Mi-25 and an MBB Bo 105.

Su-24MK serial number 24634 was the only Iraqi fighter-bomber of this type not flown to Iran in 1991. It became known as 'the Lonely' during the 1990s. (via Ali Tobchi)

On 29 November, the UN Security Council passed Resolution 678 that gave Saddam Hussein until 15 January 1991 to withdraw from Kuwait. After the war with Iran, some leading Iraqi military officers were purged from the service, but the IrAF remained generally unaffected and in a good overall condition. Once it became clear that there would be no peaceful solution to the Kuwait dispute the IrAF intensified its training, and flew a number of large-scale and very realistic exercises, some of these simulating air strikes by up to 60 aircraft against targets in Israel. MiG-25RBs also flew reconnaissance sorties into Saudi airspace, while interceptor pilots practised operations against types such as the General Dynamics F-111 and McDonnell Douglas F-15E Strike Eagle.

On 17 January 1991 a US-led coalition launched Operation Desert Storm. Knowing it was unable to match the coalition's superiority in terms of technology, equipment and training, the IrAF responded with limited activity by its interceptor units. Operations during the first 24 hours of the war yielded several unconfirmed claims for the IrAF pilots, only one of which was eventually confirmed: a MiG-25PDS flown by Capt Dawoud from No. 96 Squadron shot down a US Navy McDonnell Douglas F/A-18C Hornet. In return, the IrAF suffered the loss of four of its own fighters.

After some reorganisation and redeployments on the second day, the IrAF hit back in force on 19 January, with a combination of manned interceptors and SAMs. MiG-29s claimed one RAF Panavia Tornado as shot down, but one of them was shot down by USAF F-15 Eagles immediately afterwards. Similarly, a pair of MiG-25RBs that attempted to lure F-15s into a SAM trap was shot down due to a series of mistakes by the Iraqi ground-control interception (GCI) network. Nevertheless, during the following night, two missions by IrAF MiG-29s and MiG-25s led to a SAM kill of a USAF F-15E, and an aerial victory against a US Navy F-14A+. Even so, by now it was obvious that the IrAF could not keep on fighting and it subsequently limited its activity. Indeed, on 24 January, it began evacuating its aircraft to Iran. Only one major combat operation was launched after that day: on 30 January, two MiG-25s attempted to intercept a pair of USAF F-15s that were blocking the major evacuation route to Iran. Despite bad weather, this operation almost succeeded: although one of the MiGs managed to fire a single R-40RD missile at one of the Eagles, the USAF fighter evaded it, and the retreating Iraqis then came under a series of counterattacks by other US fighters.

A UN-negotiated ceasefire brought an end to the war, in the course of which the IrAF acknowledged the loss of 23 aircraft in the air (the US and Saudi Arabia claimed a total of 44), and 250 on the ground, while 125 aircraft were evacuated to Iran.

'No-fly' zones and the 2003 invasion

After the end of the 1991 Gulf War, the Iraqi Air Force and Iraqi Army Aviation were involved in operations against rebellions in the north and south of the country in March and April 1991. As a result of the UN sanctions following the war, the IrAF faced many problems in maintaining the operational status of its fleet, especially due to the restricted access to spare parts. Furthermore, two 'no-fly' zones (NFZ) were decreed by the coalition. The northern NFZ was extended from the 36th parallel northwards to protect the persecuted Kurdish minority (Operation Provide Comfort, followed by Operation Northern Watch in 1997). The southern NFZ was established in 1992 (Operation Southern Watch) as far as the 32nd parallel (extended to the 33rd in 1996). On 5

Different variants of the MiG-23 interceptor, here a MiG-23MS early in the war, played an increasingly important role during the late 1980s and through much of the 1990s. (Farzad Nadimi Collection)

April 1992 the IrAF scrambled fighters to intercept Iranian aircraft that were bombing bases in northern Iraq belonging to the Kurdistan Democratic Party of Iran. In 1995, several IrAF officers and pilots became involved in a coup plot against the government in Baghdad. This resulted not only in additional purges and executions, but also much-reduced Air Force activity in the years that followed.

On 27 December 1992 a MiG-25 was shot down by a USAF General Dynamics F-16 Fighting Falcon, using an AIM-120 AMRAAM air-to-air missile. This was followed by the destruction of a MiG-23 on 17 January 1993.

In August 1996, the NFZ was extended north to the 33rd parallel following the invasion of the Kurdish regions by Iraqi forces.

Starting in 1998, the IrAF launched a major attempt to revitalise its remaining fleet of combat aircraft. A number of MiG-23s, MiG-25s, MiG-29s and Mirage F.1s were overhauled, and some of them upgraded with electronic warfare systems taken from other types. The IrAF now began challenging US and UK fighters under way over southern Iraq. For example, on 5 January 1999, in two separate incidents, two pairs of MiG-25s crossed the NFZ. The subsequent aerial combat saw two USAF F-15Cs and two US Navy F-14As fire six missiles, but Iraqi fighters were able to evade them and escape back to the north.

On 30 September 2002 the IrAF became involved in another coup attempt against the government in Baghdad. A MiG-23 took off from al-Bakir for a bombing training mission. The pilot turned away toward Lake Tharthar, in order to strike Saddam Hussein's palace, but was shot down by a man-portable air defence system (MANPADS) before dropping his bombs. He was later executed together with the commanding officers at al-Bakir. On 23 December 2002, during Operation Southern Focus, a USAF RQ-1B Predator unmanned aerial vehicle (UAV), equipped with two FIM-92A Stinger missiles, was sent over Iraq, apparently to challenge Iraqi aircraft in air combat. It was first intercepted by a pair of MiG-23s that were unable to achieve a lock-on. However, a MiG-25PD that had just been scrambled was able to achieve a lock, and brought it down with a single missile.

At the beginning of 2003 the IrAF had just 71 aircraft and helicopters in service, while the Iraqi Army Aviation Corps (IrAAC) maintained a force of 37 helicopters. Four interceptor squadrons were operational: two with Chengdu F-7Bs, one with eight Mirage F.1EQs and nine MiG-29s, and one with 11 MiG-25s. In mid-March, IrAF personal were ordered to disassemble all of their aircraft. After disassembling and removing the wings, the technicians hid the aircraft around the country, covered with camouflage netting. No subsequent order was issued to reassemble the aircraft, and instead, in early March, most of the commanders were ordered to bury the aircraft in sand. Most of the aircraft were buried several kilometres outside bases or in nearby villages and towns and were then abandoned.

On 19 March 2003, four Mirage pilots attempted to launch for the only combat operation by the IrAF during the war. However, when the first of these crashed on take-off, killing its pilot – a famous veteran of the wars with Iran and over Kuwait – the mission was aborted. It was the IrAF's last ever attempt to fly a combat sortie.

AIRCRAFT OF THE 'NEW' IRAQI AIR FORCE

During the phase of occupation that followed the invasion of 2003, most Iraqi combat aircraft (by now primarily consisting of MiG-23s, MiG-25s and Su-25s) were discovered by coalition forces in poor condition on various air bases, while others were discovered buried outside their bases or in nearby towns and villages where they had been abandoned. Most IrAF aircraft were destroyed during and after the invasion, and any remaining materiel was discarded in the immediate aftermath of the war. No aircraft acquired during the era of Saddam Hussein would be retained in service by the 'new' Iraqi air arms. The Iraqi Air Force (IQAF) began to be rebuilt after the war as part of an overall programme to establish a new Iraqi defence force. When it was created in 2004, the IQAF consisted of only 35 personnel.

Today's Iraqi air arms are composed of the Iraqi Air Force (IQAF), which is equivalent to the US Air Force, and the Iraqi Army Aviation (IAA), which corresponds to US Army Aviation.

Fighter and attack aircraft

Aero Vodochody L-159 Advanced Light Combat Aircraft

The L-159 Advanced Light Combat Aircraft (ALCA) is a Czech-built multi-role combat aircraft designed for a variety of air-to-air, air-to-ground (with a wide range of NATO-standard missiles and laser-guided bombs) and reconnaissance missions, and equipped with a multi-mode pulse-Doppler Grifo-L radar for all-weather, day and night operations. The single-seat L-159 entered service in the Czech Republic in April 2000 followed by the two-seat L-159T1 version in 2007. A preliminary agreement for the supply of 28 two-seat Aero L-159T1 aircraft to Iraq was presented on 10 December 2012, including 24 newly built aircraft and four used aircraft from Czech Air Force stocks. However, this agreement was abandoned in December 2013 and new negotiations began. On 7 April 2014 the Iraqi government signed a new agreement with Aero Vodochody for the supply of 12 L-159s. On 28 August 2014 it was announced that Aero would buy back 13 single-seat L-159As and a few two-seat L-159T1 aircraft from the Czech Ministry of Defence (MoD). These would include 11 L-159As from storage and four active aircraft (two L-159As and two L-159T1s). At the time it was planned to deliver only 12 operational aircraft (10 L-159As and two L-159T1s), while the three other aircraft (two L-159As and one L-159T1) were to be used for spare parts. On 9 March 2015 the Czech government approved the sale of 15 L-159s to Iraq. Four of these were to be taken from the Czech Air Force inventory, while the remaining 11

L-159A serial number 5903 arrived at Balad AB on 5 November 2015. It was expected that the first Iraqi L-159 instructors would return to Iraq from the Czech Republic in May 2016, with three more aircraft to be received in the first half of the same year.
(Iraqi Ministry of Defense)

had been in storage for over 10 years. The aircraft were expected to be delivered in around two or three months. On 30 July 2015 the Czech Republic MoD announced that it was training 31 Iraqi helicopter pilots to fly the ALCA. In addition, preparations were being made for the training of ground personnel to maintain the aircraft once in Iraq. Further details of the contract were reported in October, including the fact that only 12 units had been ordered at a total cost of USD166.18 million including 10 L-159As at USD58.8 million; two L-159T1s at USD17.1 million; fuselage cells at USD230,000; spare parts at USD10.93 million; ground support equipment at USD5.88 million; one spare engine at USD870,000; four flight training instructors at USD5.58 million; training for eight pilots at USD10.272 million; training for 24 normal-level maintenance personnel at USD5.8432 million; training for 12 intermediate-level maintenance personnel at USD3.36 million; flight support equipment at USD2.78 million; logistical support at USD13.37 million; 12 ferry flights to Iraq by Czech pilots at USD888,000; and weapons at USD30.28 million. On arrival at Balad AB in November 2015 the aircraft formed the new 115th Squadron. On 27 February 2016 the two L-159s undertook their first sortie flown by Iraqi pilots who had completed their training in the Czech Republic.

Table 1: L-159 Aero Vodochody L-159 Advanced Light Combat Aircraft

Type	Serial no.	c/n	Delivery date	Remarks
L-159A	IQAF-5903	156049	5 November 2015	
L-159A	IQAF-5904	156055	5 November 2015	

Note: Serial numbers are applied in black, on the tail and on both sides of the fuselage below the cockpit. They are prefixed with 'IQAF'.

Cessna 208 Combat Caravan

The AC-208 Combat Caravan is a light attack combat aircraft developed by Alliant Techsystems (ATK). It is derived from the Cessna 208 Grand Caravan passenger and utility aircraft. It is fitted with AN/ALR-47 and AN/ALE-47 defensive countermeasures systems, an MX-15D turret with on-board laser designator, internal measurement unit (IMU) and micro-controller unit, and with AGM-114M/K Hellfire missiles. The AC-208B can also employ Cirit laser-guided 70mm (2.75in) rockets produced by the Turkish producer Rocketsan. By adding intelligence, surveillance and reconnaissance (ISR) equipment, ATK developed the RC-208B. The AC-208B counter-insurgency (COIN) ver-

An Iraqi AC-208 launches a Hellfire missile at a target on the Aziziyah training range, south of Baghdad, on 8 November 2010. The Iraqi airmen scored a direct hit, destroying the target in their second-ever launch of a Hellfire. (US Department of Defense)

sion was developed in 2008 as part of the US government's effort to rebuild the IQAF and was converted from the cargo/ISR aircraft. Initially integrated in the 3rd Reconnaissance Squadron, the TC-208B Grand Caravan is used for training. On 4 November 2009 the first AGM-114 Hellfire missile firing was performed by the crew of an AC-208B on a firing range near al-Assad. One year later, on 8 November 2010, the first Hellfire launch against a vehicle target was carried out on a training area at Aziziyah. With the arrival of the AC-208B the 3rd Squadron was renamed the 3rd Attack and Reconnaissance Squadron. Typical training on the Cessna 208 involved one year in the US and four months in Jordan (as confirmed by Capt M.). On 23 April 2015, Iraq received a shipment of 300 Hellfire missiles provided by the US Army Security Assistance Command (USASAC). This delivery followed Congressional notification on 22 February and a first batch of 100 missiles, along with a shipment of small arms ammunition, in the first week of March. By the end of July 2015, Cessna 208s had launched more than 1,600 Hellfire missiles.

Table 2: Cessna 208 Combat Caravan

Type	Serial no.	c/n	Delivery date	Remarks
RC-208	YI-111	208B-1226	November 2008	
RC-208	YI-112	208B-1225	November 2008	
RC-208	YI-113	208B-1227	November 2008	
TC-208	YI-114	208B-1294	29 March 2008	
TC-208	YI-115	208B-1297	14 April 2008	
TC-208	YI-116	208B-1298	23 June 2008	
AC-208	YI-117	208B-1312	12 May 2009	
AC-208	YI-118	208B-2016	23 December 2008	
AC-208	YI-119	208B-1309	9 August 2011	Shot down 16 March 2016
AC-208	YI-120			
TC-208	YI-121	208B-2014	23 December 2008	
TC-208	YI-122	208B-1132	9 August 2011	

Note: Serial numbers are applied in black on the tail.

Lockheed Martin F-16C/D Fighting Falcon

The Lockheed Martin F-16 Fighting Falcon is a single-engine multi-role fighter designed for a variety of air-to-air and air-to-ground missions. In January 2011, Iraq signed an initial contract worth USD3 billion for the acquisition of 18 F-16C/D Block 52 fighters (12 single-seat F-16Cs and six two-seat F-16Ds) for delivery between 2014 and 2015. On 12 December 2011 the US Defense Security Cooperation Agency (DSCA) notified Congress of the Iraqi government's request to purchase 18 Fighting Falcons (now designated F-16IQ) and associated equipment, parts, weapons, training and logistical support at an estimated cost of USD2.3 billion. These aircraft would have their air-to-air combat capability downgraded. Their equipment would include AN/APG-68(V)9 radars and Pratt & Whitney PW-F100-229 engines. Also ordered were 20 AN/AAQ-33 Sniper targeting pods and four Goodrich DB-110 airborne reconnaissance systems. In terms of weapons, the requests included 19 M61 Vulcan 20mm cannon, 100 AIM-9L/M-8/9 Sidewinder air-to-air missiles (AAMs), 150 AIM-7M-F1/H Sparrow AAMs, 50 AGM-65D/G/H/K Maverick air-to-ground missiles, 200 GBU-12 Paveway II laser-guided bomb (LGB) units (500lb/227kg), 50 GBU-10 Paveway II LGB units (2,000lb/907kg), 50 GBU-24 Paveway III LGB units (2,000lb/907kg), 10,000 PGU-27A/B and 30,000 PGU-28 ammunition rounds, and 230 Mk 84 2,000lb (907kg) and 800 Mk 82 500lb (227kg) bombs.

In March 2012 the first Iraqi pilot graduated from Specialized Undergraduate Pilot Training (SUPT) in the US. In October, 18 more F-16C/Ds (12 F-16Cs and six F-16Ds) were ordered for delivery between 2017 and 2018, to equip a second squadron. On 2 May 2014, the first Iraqi F-16IQ (F-16D serial number 1601) made its maiden flight at Forth Worth, Texas (piloted by Paul 'Bear' Randall with Bill 'Gigs' Gigliotti in the backseat) followed by official delivery to Iraq on 5 June. For the ceremony, this F-16D carried a full load of weapons on the wings (a Sniper pod, two AGM-65 missiles and four AIM-9L/M AAMs). After the first two aircraft to be delivered were relocated to the US Air National Guard (ANG) facility at Tucson International Airport in Arizona on 16 December, IQAF pilots began training on the two F-16Ds (serial numbers 1601 and 1602). The aircraft were temporarily assigned to the 152nd Fighter Squadron (FS), part of the Arizona ANG's 162nd Fighter Wing (FW), which operates the USAF's international F-16 training academy.

Initially, it was planned for the first F-16s to arrive at their Iraqi base in September, but the advances made by so-called Islamic State (IS) militants across the country saw this transfer suspended. In addition, Balad AB was not considered ready or adequately secure. Meanwhile, around 350 Iraqi technicians were receiving English language training in Jordan in order to handle the aircraft.

On 25 June 2015, F-16C serial number 1609 of the 162nd FW was lost together with its pilot, Brig Gen Rafid Mohammad Hassan. The probable cause of the loss was pilot vertigo during night air combat training, and the aircraft came down 8km (5 miles) east of Douglas Municipal Airport at 20.00 local time.

On 9 July two F-16Cs (serial numbers 1607 and 1610) and two F-16Ds (1601 and 1604) took off from Tucson and landed at Lajes in the Azores the same day. They landed at Balad AB on 13 July where they joined the new 9th Fighter Squadron.

F-16C serial number 1613 prepares to land at Fort Worth, Texas, in September 2015. (Carl Richards)

Table 3: Lockheed Martin F-16C/D Fighting Falcon

Type	Serial no.	c/n	Delivery date	Remarks
F-16D	1601	RB-01	5 June 2014	Assigned to 152nd FS/162nd FW on 16 December 2014; to 9th FS on 13 July 2015
F-16D	1602	RB-02		Assigned to 152nd FS/162nd FW on 16 December 2014
F-16D	1603	RB-03		Fort Worth on 17 September 2014
F-16D	1604	RB-04		Assigned to 9th FS on 13 July 2015
F-16D	1605	RB-05		Assigned to 152nd FS/162nd FW
F-16D	1606	RB-06		Fort Worth on 13 February 2015
F-16C	1607	RA-01		Assigned to 152nd FS/162nd FW on 16 December 2014; to 9th FS on 13 July 2015
F-16C	1608	RA-02		Fort Worth on 14 April 2015
F-16C	1609	RA-03		Assigned to 152nd FS/162nd FW; crashed 25 June 2015, pilot Brig Gen Rafid Mohammad Hassan KIA
F-16C	1610	RA-04		Assigned to 9th FS on 13 July 2015
F-16C	1611	RA-05		Fort Worth on 11 June 2015; assigned to 152nd FS/162nd FW
F-16C	1612	RA-06		Fort Worth on 20 September 2015; assigned to 152nd FS/162nd FW; to 9th FS on 2 February 2016
F-16C	1613	RA-07		Fort Worth on 17 September 2015
F-16C	1614	RA-08		Fort Worth on 16 September 2015; to 9th FS on 2 February 2016
F-16C	1615	RA-09		Fort Worth, February 2016
F-16C	1616	RA-10		
F-16C	1617	RA-11		Fort Worth, February 2016
F-16C	1618	RA-12		

Note: Serial numbers are applied in black on the tail. They are prefixed with 'IAF' (not 'IQAF').

Sukhoi Su-25

On 28 June 2014 the IQAF received two urgently required Su-25SMs from Russia. These were transported to New al-Muthana AB aboard an Antonov An-124. The second-hand aircraft had been operated by the Russian Air Force's 412th Aviation Base at Domna in Zabaykalsky Krai. They were previously based in East Germany with the 899th Attack Aviation Regiment. After arrival in Iraq they were quickly repaired and repainted in IQAF colours. Three more examples arrived in the next few days and were deployed to Ali AB where they were to be returned to flying condition by technicians of the 121st Aircraft Repair Plant (the aircraft comprised serial numbers 2519, 2520 and 2521). On 1 July three of the seven Su-25s operational with the Islamic Revolutionary Guards Corps Air and Space Force (IRGCASF) arrived in Baghdad: these comprised serial number 15-2459 (a Su-25UBKM delivered to IRGCASF by Ulan-Ude in January 2013), 15-2451 (a Su-25KM upgraded and modernised by Iran's Pars Aviation MRO Centre in 2011) and 15-2456 (a former Iraqi Air Force Su-25KM that had been evacuated to Iran in 1991 and then modernised in 2012). These aircraft were flown by two Iraqi and two Iranian pilots who left Mehrabad International Airport in Tehran via Ilam Airport. They seemed to have arrived at Ilam on 18 June, where Iraqi pilots conducted several training flights before transiting to al-Rashid AB in Iraq. The last four Su-25s (Su-25KM serial numbers 15-2450 and 15-2454 (ex-Iraqi), and Su-25UBKM serial numbers 15-2458 and 15-2457) arrived at al-Rashid AB the following day. In early November, a Su-25 was returned to the IRGCASF air base of Seyyed al-Shohada, followed a few days later by two Su-25UBKMs that went to Pars Aviation in Tehran for technical inspection. They still wore their Iraqi markings. On 26 March, five different Su-25s carried out air strikes from al-Rashid: the aircraft involved were former Iranian Su-25UBKM serial number 2500 and Su-25KM serial number 2513, and two former Russian Su-25SMs, serial numbers 2520 and 2522. Three others were stationed at Balad AB and the two last at al-Assad AB. On 2 April the Iraqi MoD confirmed that the IQAF had formed a new squadron to operate the Su-25s, the 109th Attack Squadron at al-Rashid AB, in the southeast of Baghdad. The type had previously been stationed at New al-Muthana AB, on the western side of Baghdad International Airport, until the end of March 2015. On 13 July a 'new' Su-25 was delivered by Iran as replacement for an aircraft lost the previous summer. The Su-25KM in question had been restored by Pars Aviation between January and June. In September, a new Su-25K recently delivered from Iran, was seen with a different colour scheme and the serial number 2502. On 20 September it was reported that Iraqi pilots were training on the Su-25 in Belarus. After completing their training in Belarus the pilots were expected to return to Iraq in a matter of weeks. The training contract was intended to increase the number of pilots able to fly the Iraqi Su-25s and to relieve the increasing pressure and fatigue on existing pilots, many of who were relative veterans. The new trainees were quickly sent to assist the existing pilots and maintain momentum during ongoing operations.

A pair of former Russian Su-25s in flight on 2 November 2014. (IQAF pilots)

Table 4: Sukhoi Su-25

Type	Serial no.	c/n	Delivery date	Remarks
Su-25KM	25xx		2 July 2014	Delivery date uncertain; formerly IRGCASF 15-2450
Su-25KM	2513	25508110291	1 July 2014	Formerly IRGCASF 15-2451
Su-25KM	25xx		2 July 2014	Formerly IrAF; IRGCASF 15-2454
Su-25KM	25xx	25508110309	1 July 2014	Formerly IrAF serial number 31; IRGCASF 12-2456
Su-25UBKM			1 July 2014	Formerly IRGCASF 15-2455
Su-25UBKM			2 July 2014	Delivery date uncertain; formerly IRGCASF 15-2457
Su-25UBKM	2500		2 July 2014	Formerly IRGCASF 15-2458
Su-25UBKM			1 July 2014	Delivery date uncertain; formerly IRGCASF 15-2459
Su-25K	2502			
Su-25SM	2518			Formerly Russian Air Force
Su-25SM	2519	25508106078	28 June 2014	Formerly Russian Air Force
Su-25SM	2520	25508103124	28 June 2014	Formerly Russian Air Force
Su-25SM	2521		July 2014	Formerly Russian Air Force
Su-25SM	2522		July 2014	Formerly Russian Air Force
Su-25KM	2504			Formerly IRGCASF

Note: In the first days after their arrival, ex-Iranian Su-25s retained their IRGCASF serial numbers, with two digits on the tail and on each side of the fuselage below the cockpit. Later they were replaced by Iraqi serial numbers, in black, on each side of the fuselage below the cockpit. They were prefixed with 'IQAF'.

Reconnaissance aircraft

Beechcraft King Air 350ER

In September 2006 the US Defense Security Cooperation Agency (DSCA) announced a possible Foreign Military Sale (FMS) to Iraq of the Raytheon Beechcraft King Air 350ER, and stated an eventual total requirement for 24 King Air 350ERs configured for intelligence, surveillance and reconnaissance (ISR) and a further 24 King Air 350ER light transport aircraft (LTA). At the time, the PZL M28 Skytruck was considered as an alternative for the LTA requirement. On 3 January 2007 the US DoD announced that a USD132.3-million FMS contract had been signed with Raytheon for five King Air 350ER ISR aircraft and one King Air 350ER LTA for the IQAF. The 350ER is a derivative of the King Air 350 with additional fuel tanks offering extended range. The ISR version is fitted with a synthetic aperture radar, datalink and L-3 Wescam MX-15 electro-optical/infrared system. Both ISR and LTA variants for the IQAF are fitted with AN/AAR-47 and AN/ALE-47 self-protection systems. The first King Air 350ER LTA version, serial number YI-150, was received on 28 December 2007 and was configured for utility and VIP transport missions, as well as for pilot training. The first King Air 350ER ISR version was delivered in April 2008 and performed ISR tasks the same month. The last of the type was received on 15 September 2009. The six aircraft were assigned to the 87th Reconnaissance Squadron based at New al-Muthana AB. On 24 March 2015 the US DoD announced that Iraq had signed a new contract for one additional Beechcraft Super King Air 350ER ISR version and one Scorpion ground station (plus one spare station) at a total cost of USD27 million. This aircraft will be delivered in March 2017.

Table 5: Beechcraft King Air 350

Type	Serial no.	c/n	Delivery date	Remarks
King Air 350ER LTA	YI-150	FL-521	28 December 2007	
King Air 350ER ISR	YI-151	FL-522	April 2008	
King Air 350ER ISR	YI-152	FL-523		
King Air 350ER ISR	YI-153	FL-530		
King Air 350ER ISR	YI-154	FL-531		
King Air 350ER ISR	YI-155	FL-533	15 September 2009	

Note: Serial numbers are applied in black on the tail.

King Air 350ER ISR serial number YI-152 at New al-Muthana AB on 24 December 2009. (Steve Kline)

Comp Air 7SLX

The Comp Air 7SLX (also known in the US as the CA-7) light aircraft is a kit plane from Aero Comp Inc., Merritt Island. The manufacturer normally builds more than 49 percent of the aircraft and the customer completes the remainder. The 7SLX is powered by a Walter M601 turboprop engine similar to the Pratt & Whitney PT6. Seven of the type were sold to the UAE, which equipped them with a reconnaissance sensor suite. A batch of four units was donated by the UAE to Iraq, soon followed by an additional batch of three. However, only six of the type were actually delivered. The first were received on 13 November 2004. They were initially operated for utility and oil pipeline surveillance, and equipped the 3rd Squadron, which received the Bell 206 one month later. On 10 April 2005 the squadron was declared operational, after the graduation of the first six pilots and eight maintenance engineers. On 30 May the IQAF lost its first aircraft since the rebirth of the air arm. A 7SLX crashed near Jalula, about 50 miles (31 miles) northeast of Baquba, during a mission from Kirkuk AB, killing five crewmembers, four US servicemen (one pilot and three ground controllers) and one Iraqi pilot. Following the crash, and after flight tests by a USAF team in October 2005, the fleet was grounded in January 2006. Aircraft c/n 2240 was shipped to the US for a complete rebuild and made its first flight at Edwards AFB, California on 25 April 2006. Plans called for the four other aircraft to be rebuilt at Kirkuk AB beginning in May 2006. The aircraft were finally withdrawn from use in late 2007. Serial numbers of the aircraft were YI-121 to YI-126.

Four of the six Comp Air 7SLX aircraft lined up at Basra International Airport in November 2004.
(US Army/SSgt Christopher J. Crawford)

Table 6: Comp Air 7SLX

Type	Serial no.	c/n	Delivery date	Remarks
7SLX	YI-12x		13 November 2004	Rebuilt in US in 2006
7SLX	YI-12x		13 November 2004	
7SLX	YI-12x		13 November 2004	
7SLX	YI-125		13 November 2004	
7SLX	YI-12x			
7SLX	YI-12x			Crashed on 30 May 2005

Note: Serial numbers were applied in black on the tail.

Pilatus U-28A

The U-28A is a modified Pilatus PC-12, first used by the USAF in Operations Enduring Freedom and Iraqi Freedom. The aircraft provides on-call/surge capability for improved tactical airborne ISR in support of special operations forces. In 2014 up to six U-28A ISR platforms were seen carrying Iraqi serial numbers. The fact that U-28s are used for intelligence gathering by the US Special Operations Command (SOCOM) suggests that the crew (two pilots, one Combat Systems Officer and one Tactical Systems Officer) are US airmen from Air Force Special Operations Command (AFSOC) and that the aircraft are drawn from the 34th, 318th and 319th Special Operations Squadron (SOS). An advantage of the U-28A in unconventional missions is that it can 'pass' for a civilian aircraft and thus go unnoticed at airports in the world's 'hot spots'. In Iraqi service these aircraft are assigned to the 62nd Utility Squadron.

Table 7: Pilatus U-28A

Type	Serial no.	c/n	Delivery date	Remarks
U-28A	YI-580		2010	
U-28A	YI-581		2010	
U-28A	YI-582		2010	
U-28A	YI-583		2010	
U-28A	YI-584		2010	
U-28A	YI-585		2010	

SAMA CH-2000

The SAMA CH-2000 is based on the design of the Zenair Zenith 2000 and is assembled by Jordan Aerospace Industries in Amman. The version in Iraqi service is the CH-2000-MTSA (Military Tactical Surveillance Aircraft), a two-seater used for surveillance and training. It is equipped with an Ultra 8500FW gyroscopic stabilisation detection system under the fuselage. This system includes an infrared imaging device and a diurnal television camera able to detect a man at 3.5km (2.2 miles) from an altitude of 600m (1,968ft). On 28 September 2004 a USD5.8-million contract for eight CH-2000s was signed by the US Army Aviation and Missile Command on behalf of Iraq, and included an option for eight more of the type. The first two units, serial numbers YI-103 and YI-104, were delivered on 18 January 2005 in Basrah. Two more aircraft were received on 21 September 2006. On 6 January 2007, Jordan Aerospace Industries announced that it had delivered the last two aircraft from the first batch. The first four aircraft joined the 3rd Squadron at Kirkuk AB, while the other four entered service with the 70th Reconnaissance Squadron at Basrah AB. In September 2009 the CH-2000 conducted manoeuvres at the Camp Wessam facility in southern Iraq together with Iraqi Army ground forces. They were used to spot simulated hostile activity, such as the placement of improvised explosive devices (IEDs), before relaying information to Army forces. On 27 June 2010 they worked together for the first time together with US Army AH-64 Apache attack helicopters. Following the arrival of the Cessna 208 in 2008, the CH-2000s were transferred from the 3rd Squadron to the 70th Reconnaissance Squadron, which relocated from Basrah to Ali AB on 17 October 2010.

CH-2000 serial number YI-106 is seen ready for its first training mission of the day. The aircraft was photographed in February 2007, while based at Kirkuk. (David Hills)

Table 8: SAMA CH-2000

Type	Serial no.	c/n	Delivery date	Remarks
CH-2000	YI-103		18 January 2005	
CH-2000	YI-104		18 January 2005	
CH-2000	YI-105		21 September 2006	
CH-2000	YI-106		21 September 2006	
CH-2000	YI-107			
CH-2000	YI-108			
CH-2000	YI-109		6 January 2007	
CH-2000	YI-110		6 January 2007	

Note: Serial numbers are applied in black on the fuselage behind the wings.

Seabird Aviation Seeker SB7L-360

The Seabird Aviation Seeker SB7L-360 is a light observation aircraft built by Seabird Aviation Australia and Seabird Aviation Jordan. Two Seekers were the first aircraft to enter service with the 'new' Iraqi Air Force. On 10 June 2004 a contract worth USD2.3 million was awarded to Seabird Aviation Jordan after an accelerated tender. The contract included training, maintenance and support. The two Seekers (serial numbers YI-101, ex-JY-SEA; and YI-102, ex-JY-SEB) were delivered on 29 July 2004, and then airlifted by a USAF C-130H from Amman to Basrah AB on 29 September. Once in Iraq they were assigned to the newly formed 70th Reconnaissance Squadron. The two aircraft received a sand-coloured camouflage and the Iraqi flag on the fin. In September 2005 they began observation missions in southern Iraq and flew an average of four hours per day and per aircraft. Their missions included monitoring supply routes and pipelines that were frequently targeted by insurgents. The Seeker is equipped with a FLIR Systems Ultra 7500 electro-optic and forward-looking infrared sensor.

Table 9: Seabird Aviation Seeker SB7L-360

Type	Serial no.	c/n	Delivery date	Remarks
SB7L-360	YI-101	920005	29 July 2004	
SB7L-360	YI-102	020006	29 July 2004	

Note: Serial numbers are applied in black on the fuselage below the tail and under the left wing.

One of the IQAF's first aircraft: Seeker SB7L-360 serial number YI-102, seen at Basrah in early August 2004.
(Dave Hedges)

Transport aircraft

Antonov An-32B

On 9 December 2009, a USD2.5-billion defence agreement was signed between Ukraine and the Iraqi MoD. The contract included 420 Khariv Morozov BTR-4 8x8 wheeled armoured personnel carriers, six Antonov ASTC/Aviant An-32B light military transport aircraft, and repair work on two Iraqi Mi-8T military helicopters. The An-32B is a light multipurpose transport that can operate in various climate conditions, including hot conditions (up to +50°C) and from mountain airfields (up to 4,500m/14,764ft) elevation). The first An-32B for the IQAF, serial number YI-401, made its first flight at Kiev-Syvatoshino, Ukraine on 9 October 2010. However, in 2011 Antonov stopped work on the six An-32Bs due to non-payment. By this stage, the first three aircraft were complete and were awaiting delivery from the factory, while two more aircraft were in production. These aircraft were initially assigned to the 23rd Transport Squadron, serving alongside the C-130 at New al-Muthana AB. Subsequently, the 33rd Transport Squadron was created in May 2013 specifically for this type of aircraft.

Table 10: Antonov An-32B

Type	Serial no.	c/n	Delivery date	Remarks
An-32B	YI-401	37-04	10 March 2012	
An-32B	YI-402	36-05	11 April 2012	
An-32B	YI-403	36-06	18 November 2011	
An-32B	YI-404	36-07	17 July 2012	
An-32B	YI-405	37-02	4 April 2012	
An-32B	YI-406	37-05	4 October 2012	

Note: Serial numbers are applied in black on the tail and under the left wing.

The first IQAF An-32B, serial number YI-403, on its arrival at New al-Muthana AB on 18 November 2011, after a flight from Kiev-Gostomel.
(Iraqi Ministry of Defense)

de Havilland Canada DHC-6 Twin Otter

The de Havilland Canada DHC-6 Twin Otter is a 19-passenger short take-off and landing (STOL) utility aircraft. In 2010, two DHC-6 aircraft were delivered to US Special Operations Command (SOCOM). Since October 2014 these two aircraft have operated from New al-Muthana AB wearing IQAF serial numbers. However, the squadron remains unknown and it is probable that these aircraft are actually assigned to SOCOM, but wear 'false' Iraqi military identities.

Table 11: de Havilland Canada DHC-6 Twin Otter

Type	Serial no.	c/n	Delivery date	Remarks
DHC-6	YI-391		October 2014?	
DHC-6	YI-392		October 2014?	

Lockheed C-130E Hercules and
Lockheed Martin C-130J Super Hercules

In 2004 the new Iraqi Air Force formulated plans to acquire two former Royal Jordanian Air Force Lockheed C-130B transports. Initial delivery of the two aircraft was planned for October 2004, and an additional four transports were to be supplied by April 2005. However, the aircraft in question were in poor condition after having been stored for 10 years at Amman. As a result, these acquisitions were abandoned. Instead, in January 2005 the 23rd Transport Squadron was reactivated at Tallil AB (which became Ali AB only a few months later) with the receipt of three former USAF C-130E Hercules. The 23rd Transport Squadron had originally been activated on 14 July 1965, at al-Rashid. The three C-130Es were built between 1962 and 1963 and had relatively few flight hours compared with other C-130s of the same era: 25,075 for YI-301, 23,500 for YI-302 and 20,150 for YI-303. About 65 members of the IQAF including four crews received an intensive four-month period of training in Jordan and at Tallil AB from the 23rd Advisory Support Team, part of the USAF's 777th Expeditionary Airlift Squadron, from Little Rock AFB, Arkansas. On 31 January 2006 the squadron moved to New

C-130E serial number YI-302 is a former US Air Force Hercules with 23,500 flight hours at the time of its delivery to Iraq. (Steve Kline)

C-130J-30 serial number YI-304 during its maiden flight at Lockheed Martin's plant in Marietta on 16 August 2012. (Lockheed Martin/John Rossino)

al-Muthana AB near Baghdad. On 30 September 2009 the IQAF began fully independent C-130E operations, marking the end of the air advisory mission by the USAF's 321st Air Expeditionary Advisory Squadron.

On 30 April 2009 Iraq ordered four C-130J-30 Super Hercules from Lockheed Martin in Marietta, Georgia, at a cost of USD292.8 million, and two more examples were added on 11 August. The agreement also covered spare parts, support equipment and training of pilots and mechanics by the Rhode Island Air National Guard's 143rd Airlift Wing/143rd Airlift Squadron at Quonset ANGB, North Kingstown. The first Iraqi C-130J-30, serial number YI-304, made its maiden flight at Lockheed Martin's plant in Marietta on 16 August 2012. The first three examples were delivered at Marietta before the end of the year. A first C-130J departed Marietta on 23 April 2013 and the last three examples arrived at New al-Muthana AB the following month.

Table 12: Lockheed C-130 Hercules and Lockheed Martin C-130J Super Hercules

Type	Serial no.	c/n	Delivery date	Remarks
C-130E	YI-301	382-3802	16 January 2005	Formerly USAF 62-1839
C-130E	YI-302	382-3789	16 January 2005	Formerly USAF 62-1826
C-130E	YI-303	382-3903	16 January 2005	Formerly USAF 63-7826
C-130J-30	YI-304	382-5702	14 December 2012	
C-130J-30	YI-305	382-5703	14 December 2012	
C-130J-30	YI-306	382-5704	14 December 2012	
C-130J-30	YI-307	382-5720	6 May 2013	
C-130J-30	YI-308	382-5721	6 May 2013	
C-130J-30	YI-309	382-5722	6 May 2013	

Note: Serial numbers are applied in black on the tail.

Training aircraft

Beechcraft T-6A Texan II

In August 2009 the Hawker Beechcraft Corporation received a contract for eight T-6A Texan II training aircraft for the Iraqi Air Force, followed by another order for seven additional units in September. The overall package included ground-based training systems, spares parts, logistics support and maintenance. On 16 December 2009, simultaneous with the delivery of the first batch of four T-6As, the Iraqi Flight Training School became the Iraqi Air Force College, and moved to Combat Operating Base (COB) Speicher, near Tikrit. The initial four aircraft equipped the 3rd Training Squadron. The final batch of four aircraft left the US on 8 November 2010 and arrived in Iraq the following day, coinciding with the first graduation of 20 new Iraqi pilots (eight on fixed-wing and 12 on rotary-wing types), bringing the total number of pilots trained to 102 (55 fixed-wing and 47 rotary-wing). Initial flight training on the T-6A began on 20 March 2010, under the instruction of US Air Force airmen from the 52nd Expeditionary Flying Training Squadron (EFTS). In January 2011, the 3rd Training Squadron was renamed as the 203rd Training Squadron. On 5 September 2011, 11 trained Iraqi instructors took on the role of the US instructors, whose mission was now complete.

T-6A serial numbers YI-504 and YI-505 during a training flight near Tikrit, operated by advisors of the USAF's 52nd Expeditionary Flying Training Squadron.
(USAF)

Table 13: Beechcraft T-6A Texan II

Type	Serial no.	c/n	Delivery date	Remarks
T-6A Texan II	YI-501	PT496	16 December 2009	
T-6A Texan II	YI-502	PT497	16 December 2009	
T-6A Texan II	YI-503	PT498	3 February 2010	
T-6A Texan II	YI-504	PT499	16 December 2009	
T-6A Texan II	YI-505	PT500	16 December 2009	
T-6A Texan II	YI-506	PT501	3 February 2010	
T-6A Texan II	YI-507	PT502	3 February 2010	
T-6A Texan II	YI-508	PT503	3 February 2010	
T-6A Texan II	YI-509	PT512	21 September 2010	
T-6A Texan II	YI-510	PT513	21 September 2010	
T-6A Texan II	YI-511	PT514	21 September 2010	
T-6A Texan II	YI-512	PT515	9 November 2010	
T-6A Texan II	YI-513	PT516	9 November 2010	
T-6A Texan II	YI-514	PT517	9 November 2010	
T-6A Texan II	YI-515	PT518	9 November 2010	

Note: Serial numbers are applied in black behind the canopy.

Cessna 172S Skyhawk SP

The Iraqi Flight Training School opened its doors on 1 October 2007, in Kirkuk. Work to restore the base following the coalition bombing campaign of 2003 took around two years. The opening of the Iraqi Flight Training School coincided with the arrival of the first two Cessna 172S from a batch of 12 that had been ordered on 8 March 2003, via the US Air Force Materiel Command (the agreement also included an option for another 10 aircraft). The first two aircraft, serial numbers YI-131 and YI-132, arrived in Iraq on 19 October 2007. The USAF's 52nd Expeditionary Flying Training Squadron (EFTS) conducted initial training on the type. Beginning in March 2008, four more Cessna 172S aircraft were delivered, these comprising serial numbers YI-133, YI-134, YI-135 and YI-136. One of the aircraft in the next batch, serial number YI-138, was forced to make an emergency landing on a highway in Florida on 20 January 2008 after an engine failure. Serial numbers YI-137 and YI-138 arrived at Kirkuk in mid-March. All these aircraft were assigned to the 1st Training Squadron. In March 2009, the last two Skyhawks, serial numbers YI-141 and YI-142, were delivered to the IQAF. In March 2011, the 1st Training Squadron was renamed as the 201st Training Squadron. Iraqi student pilots fly the Skyhawk for 90 hours over a period of six months.

Table 14: Cessna 172S Skyhawk SP

Type	Serial no.	c/n	Delivery date	Remarks
Cessna 172S Skyhawk SP	YI-131	172SS-10464	19 October 2007	
Cessna 172S Skyhawk SP	YI-132	172SS-10465	19 October 2007	
Cessna 172S Skyhawk SP	YI-133	172SS-10565	March 2008	
Cessna 172S Skyhawk SP	YI-134	172SS-10573	March 2008	
Cessna 172S Skyhawk SP	YI-135	172SS-10579	March 2008	
Cessna 172S Skyhawk SP	YI-136	172SS-10551	March 2008	
Cessna 172S Skyhawk SP	YI-137	172SS-10646	March 2008	
Cessna 172S Skyhawk SP	YI-138	172SS-10647	March 2008	Emergency landing on 20 January 2008 after an engine failure
Cessna 172S Skyhawk SP	YI-139	172SS-10798	3 December 2008	
Cessna 172S Skyhawk SP	YI-140	172SS-10799	3 December 2008	
Cessna 172S Skyhawk SP	YI-141	172SS-10811	March 2009	
Cessna 172S Skyhawk SP	YI-142	172SS-10819	March 2009	

Note: Serial numbers are applied in black on the tail.

Cessna 172S Skyhawk SP serial number YI-140 arrived at Kirkuk AB in December 2008. (Steve Kline)

Lasta 95N with Iraqi serial number YI-173 during a test flight at the UTVA factory in Batanica in 2011.
(Igor Salinger)

Lasta-95N

In December 2007, Iraq ordered 20 examples of the Lasta-95N from the Serbian aircraft manufacturer UTVA. In November 2009 the first Iraqi Lasta-95N made its maiden flight at Batajnica air base, 10 months after the first Serbian prototype had flown. These training aircraft can carry weapons on two pylons, including pods armed with machine guns of 7.62 and 12.7mm (0.3 and 0.5in) calibre and bombs of up to 100kg (220lb). The first six aircraft were delivered to Iraq in August 2010; the final aircraft was delivered in March 2011. In the meantime, eight Iraqi pilots twice visited the Technical Test Centre at the Batajnica airport for flight tests. They later became the first flying instructors on this aircraft in Iraq. The Lasta-95Ns initially joined the 202nd Training Squadron. After several months of test flights, in February 2012 a total of 200 cadets began training on the aircraft at Tikrit AB, home of the Air Force College. However, only a month later, after a total of 600 flight hours, the fleet was grounded due to a problem with the Lycoming AEIO-580-B1A engines. Solving this problem, together with a modification of the flight controls, began in mid-May 2013 and was undertaken by teams of engineers and technicians from the UTVA factory. In July 2014 an Iraqi Ministry of Defense (MoD) video showed the Lasta-95N in flight in the Saqlawiyah area, where Iraqi forces were engaged in combat against the so-called Islamic State, but it cannot be confirmed whether the aircraft were flying reconnaissance or attack missions.

Table 15: UTVA Lasta-95N

Type	Serial no.	c/n	Delivery date	Remarks
Lasta-95N	YI-160		5 August 2010	
Lasta-95N	YI-161		5 August 2010	
Lasta-95N	YI-162		5 August 2010	
Lasta-95N	YI-163		25 August 2010	
Lasta-95N	YI-164		25 August 2010	
Lasta-95N	YI-165		25 August 2010	
Lasta-95N	YI-166			
Lasta-95N	YI-167			
Lasta-95N	YI-168			
Lasta-95N	YI-169			
Lasta-95N	YI-170			
Lasta-95N	YI-171			
Lasta-95N	YI-172			
Lasta-95N	YI-173			
Lasta-95N	YI-174			
Lasta-95N	YI-175			
Lasta-95N	YI-176			
Lasta-95N	YI-177			
Lasta-95N	YI-178			
Lasta-95N	YI-179		March 2011	

Note: Serial numbers are applied in black on the rear fuselage behind the canopy.

AIRCRAFT OF IRAQI ARMY AVIATION

Attack aircraft

Mil Mi-28NE

The Mi-28NE 'Night Hunter' is an attack helicopter designed to carry out search and destroy operations against tanks, armoured and unarmoured vehicles, and enemy personnel in combat, as well as low-speed airborne targets. It can operate night and day, and in adverse weather conditions. Between April and August 2012, Iraq signed contracts with Russia for 30 Mi-28NE helicopters, an unknown number of Igla-S (SA-24) man-portable air defence systems and 50 Pantsir-S1 gun/missile short-range air defence systems. On 10 November 2012 a temporary suspension of the deal was announced after the discovery of apparent corruption. On 16 April 2013 Rostec Director General Sergey Chemezov and Rosneft President Igor Sechin signed a new contract for six Mi-35M helicopters during a visit to Iraq. Renewed negotiations relating to the previous deal ultimately resulted in an order for 28 Mi-35M and 15 Mi-28NE helicopters in mid-2013 (the six Mi-35s ordered on 16 April 2013 were included in this new deal). On 2 July 2014 the first Iraqi Mi-28NE was spotted at the Rostov-on-Don manufacturing plant. On 25 August the first photographs emerged of a Mi-28NE ready to be conveyed from Rostov-on-Don to Iraq. Once in Baghdad they were quickly assigned to a new

Mi-28NE serial number YI-803 seen at al-Taji AB on 10 June 2015. The N025 Almaz-280 millimetre-wave radar is mounted above the main rotor. (IAA pilots)

unit, the 28th Attack Squadron, based at New al-Muthana AB, and received the serial numbers YI-281, YI-282 and YI-283. On 13 September the Iraqi MoD released an official video of a first Mi-28NE fully assembled and undergoing flight-testing before a debut operational mission. In January 2015 the serial numbers of the first aircraft were changed to YI-802, YI-803 and YI-805. Since the beginning of 2015, most Mi-28s and Mi-35s have been based at al-Kut AB in southern Iraq, with only three Mi-28NEs operational at al-Taji (YI-802, YI-803 and YI-805). Their home base was changed for security reasons since after several attacks launched against New al-Muthana AB and Baghdad IAP by infiltrated IS militants from late 2014 to early 2015.

Table 16: Mil Mi-28NE

Type	Serial no.	c/n	Delivery date	Remarks
Mi-28NE	YI-802		26 August 2014	
Mi-28NE	YI-803		26 August 2014	
Mi-28NE	YI-805		26 August 2014	
Mi-28NE	YI-806		1 February 2015	
Mi-28NE	YI-807		26 August 2015	
Mi-28NE	YI-811		1 February 2015	
Mi-28NE	YI-xxx		26 August 2015	
Mi-28NE	YI-xxx		26 August 2015	
Mi-28NE	YI-xxx		26 August 2015	
Mi-28NE	YI-xxx		6 September 2015	
Mi-28NE	YI-xxx		6 September 2015	
Mi-28NE	YI-xxx		10 December 2015	
Mi-28NE	YI-xxx		10 December 2015	

Note: Serial numbers are applied in black on both sides of the fuselage behind the wings.

Mil Mi-35M

The multi-role Mi-35M attack helicopter represents a comprehensive modernisation of the Mi-24V. In Iraqi service it can carry weapons including eight Ataka-V anti-tank missiles and launchers for S-8 rockets. A nose turret carries a GSh-23-1 23mm two-barrel cannon. The cockpit and vital components of the helicopter are significantly armoured. Alongside the 15 Mi-28 helicopters mentioned above, Iraq placed an order for 28 Mi-35M assault helicopters in mid-2013, to which were added six Mi-35Ms previously ordered on 16 April 2013. By 6 November 2013 the first batch of four Mi-35Ms was ready to be delivered from Rostov-on-Don. These were assigned to the 35th Attack Squadron after delivery by ship to the port city of Umm Qasr. In May 2014 a second batch of four Mi-35s was delivered to New al-Muthana AB. Iraqi pilots received training at the Russian base of Torzhok. Mi-35M pilot Capt M. described conducting eight months of training in Russia and three months in Iraq.

Table 17: Mil Mi-35M

Type	Serial no.	c/n	Delivery date	Remarks
Mi-35M	YI-351		2 December 2013	
Mi-35M	YI-352		2 December 2013	Crashed 16 June 2014
Mi-35M	YI-353		2 December 2013	
Mi-35M	YI-354		2 December 2013	
Mi-35M	YI-355		28 May 2014	
Mi-35M	YI-356		28 May 2014	Shot down 3 October 2014
Mi-35M	YI-357		28 May 2014	
Mi-35M	YI-358		28 May 2014	
Mi-35M	YI-359		27 September 2014	
Mi-35M	YI-360		27 September 2014	
Mi-35M	YI-361		27 September 2014	Hard landing west of Samarra after hitting power line
Mi-35M	YI-362		27 September 2014	
Mi-35M	YI-363		2 July 2015	
Mi-35M	YI-364		2 July 2015	
Mi-35M	YI-365		2 July 2015	
Mi-35M	YI-366		2 July 2015	
Mi-35M	YI-xxx		26 August 2015	
Mi-35M	YI-xxx		26 August 2015	
Mi-35M	YI-xxx		26 August 2015	
Mi-35M	YI-xxx		26 August 2015	

Note: Serial numbers are applied in black on both sides of the fuselage behind the wings.

Mi-35M serial number YI-354 seen at al-Kut AB on 1 August 2015. It is equipped with an S-8 rocket launcher and a single empty Ataka ATGM launcher on its right stub-wing.
(IAA pilots)

Armed reconnaissance aircraft

Bell IA-407

The Iraqi Armed 407 (IA-407) is an armed scout helicopter similar to the ARH-70 developed for the US Army but cancelled in October 2008. It is equipped with a turret under the nose containing a FLIR, optical camera and laser telemetry and target designation equipment. It can be armed with 12.7mm (0.5in) machine gun pods and rocket launchers. On 18 February 2009 the first three IA-407 helicopters were ordered from Bell Helicopters Textron Inc. of Forth Worth, Texas. These three units were used as prototypes for testing and development of military modifications for the IA-407. In April 2009, Bell Helicopters announced a USD60.3-million contract for 24 Bell 407s for Iraq, in addition to the three trainers. The first three of the type were delivered as T-407 training versions and arrived at al-Taji AB on 11 December 2010 on board a USAF C-17. On 10 April 2012, Bell Helicopters received a contract to supply the Iraqi Army with 30 Bell 407 helicopters (the two contracts for three T-407s ordered in February 2009 and 24 IA-407s ordered in April 2009 were thus modified to create one contract of 30 units.) The IA-407 entered service with the 21st Armed Reconnaissance Squadron. In January 2014 three additional helicopters brought total deliveries to 30 units. In May 2015 a new batch of five units was delivered according to an unknown contract, and probably to replace aircraft lost or damaged in combat. By this date, Iraq had received 51 Bell 407s including two units that were lost and 16 Bell 407GX aircraft serving with the Army Aviation College. The 21st Squadron uses a total of 33 helicopters of the type, but not all are operational simultaneously and some may be used for spare parts.

Table 18: Bell IA-407

Type	Serial no.	c/n	Delivery date	Remarks
IA-407	YI-111	53865		Formerly 09-00111
IA-407	YI-112	53890		Formerly 09-00112
IA-407	YI-113	53912		Formerly 09-00113
IA-407	YI-114	53927		Formerly 09-00114
IA-407	YI-115	53982		Formerly 09-00115
IA-407	YI-116	53983		Formerly 09-00116
IA-407	YI-117	53997		Formerly 09-00117
IA-407	YI-118	54003		Formerly 09-00118
IA-407	YI-119	54009		Formerly 09-00119
IA-407	YI-120	54015		Formerly 09-00120
IA-407	YI-121	54021		Formerly 09-00121
IA-407	YI-122	54026		Formerly 09-00122
IA-407	YI-123	54028		Formerly 09-00123
IA-407	YI-124	54029		Formerly 09-00124
IA-407	YI-125	54030		Formerly 09-00125; shot down on 28 September 2015
IA-407	YI-126	54031		Formerly 09-00126
IA-407	YI-127	54032		Formerly 09-00127
IA-407	YI-128	54033		Formerly 09-00128
IA-407	YI-129	54034		Formerly 09-00129

Bell IA-407 serial number YI-113 equipped with a 12.7mm machine gun pod and a Hydra 70 rocket launcher, and seen on 25 October 2011. (Iraqi Ministry of Defense)

IA-407	YI-130	54035		Formerly 09-00130
IA-407	YI-131	54036		Formerly 09-00131
IA-407	YI-132	54037		Formerly 09-00132
IA-407	YI-133	54039		Formerly 09-00133
IA-407	YI-134	54040		Formerly 09-00134
IA-407	YI-135	54041		Formerly 09-00135
IA-407	YI-136	54042	14 January 2013	Formerly 09-00136
IA-407	YI-137	54043		Formerly 09-00137
T-407	YI-138	53979	11 December 2010	Formerly 09-00138
T-407	YI-139	53980	11 December 2010	Formerly 09-00139
T-407	YI-140	53981	11 December 2010	Formerly 09-00140
IA-407	YI-141	54149	May 2015	Formerly 12-01141
IA-407	YI-142	54150	May 2015	Formerly 12-01142
IA-407	YI-143	54151	May 2015	Formerly 12-01143
IA-407	YI-144	54152	May 2015	Formerly 12-01144
IA-407	YI-145	54153	May 2015	Formerly 12-01145

Note: Serial numbers are applied in black in small digits on the tail below the Iraqi flag. The three digits of the serial number are also applied in black on the front of the nose.

Bell T-407 serial number YI-138 photographed on 14 July 2011 at al-Taji AB where the 721st Air Expeditionary Advisory Squadron trained, advised and assisted Iraqi pilots and maintenance personnel. (USAF/SSgt Mike Meares)

Eurocopter EC635T2+ and EC135P2+

The Eurocopter EC635 s a multi-purpose light helicopter developed by Eurocopter as a military version of the Eurocopter EC135. On 25 March 2009, French and Iraqi defence ministers signed an agreement to validate a contract signed some time previously with Eurocopter (probably during the visit of French President Nicolas Sarkozy to Iraq in February). This USD488-million deal included 24 EC635T2+ helicopters, pilot training, maintenance and support given, including provision of Gazelle helicopters to train Iraqi pilots in France. On 9 November 2009, EC635T2+ serial number YI-293 made its first flight, followed by YI-270 on 7 December. In 2010, Eurocopter (today Airbus Helicopters) announced plans to integrated Denel Dynamics Ingwe anti-tank missiles on to the type as part of the Stand-Alone Weapon System (SAWS) kit. A first helicopter, YI-293, was then sent to South Africa. The first flight tests with the Nexter NC-621 20mm cannon pod and FN Herstal HMP-400 12.7mm (0.5in) gun pod were performed

Seen on 14 June 2014, EC635 serial number YI-274 was taking of from al-Taji AB to conduct air raids around Samarra and in the provinces of Nineveh and Salah ad-Din. It is armed with the FN Herstal HMP-400 machine gun pod.
(Iraqi Ministry of Defense)

the same year. The EC635 can also be armed with FZ-233 70mm (2.75in) rocket launchers. The first two helicopters were delivered to Iraq on 8 May 2011, arriving at al-Taji AB, followed by two more a month later. Another batch of four units was received in October and one more helicopter arrived in December. In December 2011 the first firing tests of the Ingwe missile were performed aboard an EC635 by Advanced Technologies and Engineering (ATE, later Paramount Advanced Technologies) at the Murray Hill Test Range near Pretoria. The two last units, YI-290 and YI-291, were delivered in June 2012, but an additional aircraft, YI-292, was then seen in May 2015. From early August, Iraqi EC635s added the Ingwe missile to its range of weapons. A number of EC635s and Bell IA-407s are used for VIP transport, filming and imaging, and in October 2015, Defence Minister Khaled al-Obeidi used EC135P2+ serial number YI-294 for a VIP flight. One EC635 (serial number YI-2xx) has been converted to become an air ambulance by Airbus Helicopters.

Table 19: Eurocopter EC635T2+ and EC135P2+

Type	Serial no.	c/n	Delivery date	Remarks
EC635T2+	YI-270	0869		
EC635T2+	YI-271	0931 or 0935		
EC635T2+	YI-272	0949		
EC635T2+	YI-273	0958		
EC635T2+	YI-274	0968		
EC635T2+	YI-275	0975		
EC635T2+	YI-276	0980		
EC635T2+	YI-277	0983		
EC635T2+	YI-278	0988		
EC635T2+	YI-279	0992		
EC635T2+	YI-280	0995		
EC635T2+	YI-281	1002		
EC635T2+	YI-282	1005		
EC635T2+	YI-283	1009		
EC635T2+	YI-284	1015		
EC635T2+	YI-285	1018		
EC635T2+	YI-286	1023		
EC635T2+	YI-287	1026		
EC635T2+	YI-288	1032		
EC635T2+	YI-289	1035	June 2012	
EC635T2+	YI-290	1038	June 2012	
EC635T2+	YI-291			
EC635T2+	YI-292	0944		
EC635T2+	YI-293	1041		
EC135P2+	YI-294	1090		Seen October 2015; VIP

Note: Serial numbers are applied in black on the tail below the rotor. Most aircraft have a large Iraqi flag above the serial number. A small number of aircraft have a smaller flag with the serial number applied between the flag and the rotor (YI-270 to YI-275).

Transport and special operations aircraft

Bell UH-1H Huey II

In 2004, Jordan donated 16 former Royal Jordanian Air Force UH-1Hs to Iraq. The first two examples were delivered al-Taji AB on 1 February 2005 and the others followed in the course of 2006. The first batch of eight aircraft was assigned to the 2nd Utility Squadron and the second batch to the 4th Transport Squadron. Initially, their primary missions were coastal patrol, troop transport and rescue. In late 2005 modernization to Huey II standard was planned, with work to be undertaken by US Helicopter Inc. at Ozark, Alabama. The first five aircraft were re-delivered to Iraq in February 2007. They were equipped with armoured protection and a 7.62mm (0.3in) machine gun in the door. On 14 May 2008 a Huey II flew a medical evacuation mission from the Air Force Theater Hospital at Balad AB to the US Army's 86th Combat Support Hospital in Baghdad. In 2015 two new UH-1Hs were reportedly delivered.

Table 20: Bell UH-1H Huey II

Type	Serial no.	c/n	Delivery date	Remarks
UH-1H	YI-201	10500	1 February 2005	
UH-1H	YI-202	11279	1 February 2005	
UH-1H	YI-203	11132		
UH-1H	YI-204	10225		
UH-1H	YI-205	05575		
UH-1H	YI-206	10406		
UH-1H	YI-207	05461		
UH-1H	YI-208	04397		
UH-1H	YI-209	10942		
UH-1H	YI-210	09165		
UH-1H	YI-211	05268		

UH-1H Huey II serial number YI-214 during a training exercise. (USAF)

UH-1H	YI-212	08638	
UH-1H	YI-214	10850	
UH-1H	YI-215	10654	
UH-1H	YI-216	11145	
UH-1H	YI-217	10072	
UH-1H	YI-218		2015?
UH-1H	YI-219		2015?

Note: Serial numbers are applied in black on the tail. The three digits of the serial number are also applied in sand colour on the front of the nose.

Two UH–1H Huey II helicopters during Army Day celebrations on 6 January 2008. Iraq celebrated its 87th Army Day with a military parade. (US Army)

Mil Mi-8, Mi-17 and Mi-171

The IQAF formerly operated six Mi-8T transport helicopters. In December 2009 the Sevastopol Aircraft Plant in Ukraine refurbished two Iraqi Mi-8Ts as part of the BTR-4/An-32 contract. These two units probably comprised two former Iraqi Airways aircraft that had previously been seen in good condition: YI-APN in 2005, and YI-APM in 2010. These helicopters were initially operated by the 4th Squadron, IAA. They were later transferred to the 16th Training Squadron (see Training aircraft, later in this chapter).

Table 21: Mil Mi-8T

Type	Serial no.	c/n	Delivery date	Remarks
Mi-8T	YI-571			Seen July 2007
Mi-8T	YI-572			Seen July 2011 at Sevastopol Aircraft Plant (Ukraine)
Mi-8T	YI-APM	99257173		Formerly Iraqi Airways
Mi-8T	YI-APN	99257245	2005	Formerly Iraqi Airways

Note: Serial numbers are applied in black on the tail boom.

Mi-8T serial number YI-572 was seen on 19 July 2011 at the Sevastopol Aircraft Plant, Ukraine.
(Yuriy Chikhranov)

Following the rejection of a first batch of 24 second-hand Mi-17V-1 (Mi-8MTV-1) helicopters ordered from the Polish BUMAR group in December 2004, the Iraqi MoD ordered 10 new Mi-17V-5 (Mi-8MTV-5) aircraft from BUMAR in February 2005, with the contractor also responsible for maintenance and training. The order included seven helicopters produced by Kazan and three from Ulan-Ude; one of the Mi-17s was configured for VIP transport. On 14 February 2006 the first four Mi-17s arrived at New al-Muthana AB aboard an An-124, followed by a second batch of four delivered on 17 February. Around the same time, Iraq apparently received three other VIP-configured Mi-17s. Two other Mi-17s were delivered later that year. They subsequently transferred to al-Taji AB, 24km (15 miles) north of Baghdad, to operate with the 4th Transport Squadron. One of these aircraft crashed on 4 March 2008. On 3 November 2008 a first batch of four Mi-17V-5 helicopters to equip the 15th Special Operations Squadron were received at al-Taji; total Mi-17V-5 deliveries amounted to 19, including the four VIP machines. On

Two Iraqi Mi-17V-5s – serial numbers YI-262 (foreground) and YI-269 – stand by for an aeromedical evacuation mission from the Air Force Theater Hospital at Balad AB.
(USAF/Airman 1st Class Jason Epley)

3 December 2008 the Mi-17 conducted a night mission over Baghdad, the two crew-members using night vision equipment. This was the first ever Mi-17 night vision goggle (NVG) sortie outside al-Taji AB (a first NVG sortie had occurred in August). The first part of the mission saw the helicopter fly to the Besmaya range for NVG gunnery training for gunners and pilots, after which the helicopter landed first at Landing Zone Washington, in Baghdad's International Zone, then at Landing Zone Liberty, near Baghdad International Airport.

On 7 March 2009, Aeronautical Radio Incorporated (ARINC) of Annapolis, Maryland received a USD80.6-million contract for 22 Mi-17CT (CT for counter-terrorism) helicopters (modified Mi-171Es) in support of the Iraqi government. Work was performed at Warner Robins, Georgia (15 percent), Airfreight Aviation Ltd in Sharjah, UAE (20 percent) and Ulan-Ude Aviation Plant, Russia (65 percent). The first two Mi-17CTs were delivered to Iraq in May 2010. On 16 June 2011 the last two of 22 Mi-17CTs arrived at al-Taji AB.

Table 22: Mil Mi-17V-5

Type	Serial no.	c/n	Delivery date	Remarks
Mi-17V-5	YI-251	784 M11		
Mi-17V-5	YI-252	784 M12		
Mi-17V-5	YI-253	784 M13		
Mi-17V-5	YI-254	784 M14		VIP version
Mi-17V-5	YI-255			
Mi-17V-5	YI-256			
Mi-17V-5	YI-257			
Mi-17V-5	YI-258			
Mi-17V-5	YI-259	171E00054402401U		
Mi-17V-5	YI-260	171E00054402402U		
Mi-17V-5	YI-261	171E00067842309U	2 March 2007	
Mi-17V-5	YI-262	171E00067842310U	4 March 2007	
Mi-17V-5	YI-263	171E00064402403U		
Mi-17V-5	YI-264	171E00064402404U		
Mi-17V-5	YI-265			
Mi-17V-5	YI-266			
Mi-17V-5	YI-267			
Mi-17V-5	YI-268			Crashed on 28 July 2010
Mi-17V-5	YI-269			

Note: Serial numbers are applied in black on the tail boom.

Table 23: Mil Mi-17CT (Mi-171E)

Type	Serial no.	c/n	Delivery date*	Remarks
Mi-171E		171E00784073604U	29 April 2009	
Mi-171E		171E00784073605U	29 April 2009	
Mi-171E		171E00784073606U	29 April 2009	
Mi-171E		171E00784073607U	29 April 2009	

Mi-171E	171E00784083608U	2 June 2009
Mi-171E	171E00784083609U	2 June 2009
Mi-171E	171E00784083610U	2 June 2009
Mi-171E	171E00784083701U	2 June 2009
Mi-171E	171E00784083702U	4 August 2009
Mi-171E	171E00784083703U	4 August 2009
Mi-171E	171E00784083704U	4 August 2009
Mi-171E	171E00784083705U	4 August 2009
Mi-171E	171E00784083706U	12 August 2009
Mi-171E	171E00784083707U	12 August 2009
Mi-171E	171E00784083708U	12 August 2009
Mi-171E	171E00784083709U	12 August 2009
Mi-171E	171E00784083710U	19 August 2009
Mi-171E	171E00784083801U	19 August 2009
Mi-171E	171E00784083802U	19 August 2009
Mi-171E	171E00784083803U	19 August 2009
Mi-171E	171E00784083804U	2 September 2009
Mi-171E	171E00784083805U	2 September 2009

* Delivery date to factory before upgrade to CT version.
Note: Serial numbers are applied in black on the tail boom.

A rare photograph of Mi-171E serial number 420 carrying a Russian-made 500kg (1,102lb) FAB-500M-62 free-fall bomb at an unknown location in Iraq. The weapon likely originated from Belarusian stocks.

On 11 July 2010 two Mi-171E transport helicopters were delivered to the IAA at al-Taji AB. These represented the last aircraft out of an order for eight that were intended to strengthen the country's military before the withdrawal of American troops at the end of 2011. All IQAF helicopters had been transferred to the Army's control at the beginning of 2009. The first two new Mi-171Es from a second batch of 14 arrived at al-Taji around mid-November, followed on 16 and 23 January 2011 by four helicopters and by four more in April. Two more were delivered on 8 May. This delivery provided for a total of 12 of the 14 helicopters ordered the year before and the aircraft entered

service with the 15th SOS. The final two units arrived in June. The Army thus ordered 22 Mi-171Es and 22 Mi-17CT helicopters.

In October 2012 new weapons and attack, navigation and fire-control systems were integrated on two Mi-17V-5s (including YI-265) by the Serbian company Yugoimport-SDPR. The work had begun the previous February. The upgrade included new pylons and adaptor rails to carry 57mm (2.24in) rocket launchers, Serbian-made M08 pods (with Zastava M87 12.7mm/0.5in machine gun) or M09 pods (with Zastava M55-09 20mm cannon) and the main pylons were also widened to carry four Malyutka-2N/F missiles. New sensors were mounted under the nose (CCD TV, thermal cameras and laser rangefinder) and the pilots benefited from a fully digital flight control system. Thirteen other aircraft were subsequently upgraded after the first examples had been delivered to their units.

Seen at Batajnica in October 2012, this is one of the two Mi-17V-5s that were used to test new equipment under a Serbian-made modification. (Igor Salinger)

Table 24: Mil Mi-171E

Type	Serial no.	c/n	Delivery date	Remarks
Mi-171E	YI-401			
Mi-171E	402			
Mi-171E	YI-403			Assigned to 4th Squadron
Mi-171E	404			
Mi-171E	405			
Mi-171E	406			
Mi-171E	407			
Mi-171E	408		November 2010	
Mi-171E	409			
Mi-171E	410			
Mi-171E	411			
Mi-171E	412			
Mi-171E	413			
Mi-171E	414			
Mi-171E	415		20 April 2011	Crashed on 3 February 2015
Mi-171E	416		20 April 2011	
Mi-171E	417		27 April 2011	Crashed on 9 May 2013
Mi-171E	418		27 April 2011	
Mi-171E	419		8 June 2011	
Mi-171E	420			
Mi-171E	421		15 June 2011	
Mi-171E	422			

Note: Serial numbers are applied in black on the tail boom.

In November 2014 eight new Mi-171Sh helicopters were delivered by An-124 in accordance with a contract signed in 2012. First, they were integrated within the 4th and 15th Squadrons, pending the arrival of a new batch of four units in December. Iraq ultimately ordered 60 of the type. In future, they will be assigned to four separate squadrons, three of which will be newly established. By the end of 2015, a total of 87 Mi-8/17/171 aircraft had been delivered to the IAA; 16 of them were lost between

Mi-171E serial numbers 418 and 421 made their way over the city of Ramadi, and the Euphrates River, to touch down at the helicopter landing zone at Camp Ramadi on 15 November 2011.
(US Army/SSgt Nancy Lugo)

2008 and 2014, and one was lost the following year. By 2015 the 15th SOS operated a dozen Mi-171Sh aircraft, the last of its Mi-17V-5s and Mi-171Es having been transferred respectively to the Army Aviation College (16th and 85th Training Squadrons) and the 4th Transport Squadron. The 4th Squadron retained only the Mi-171E in service and transferred its last Mi-17V-5 to the Army Aviation College too. In July 2015 two new Mi-171Sh aircraft and one VIP-configured Mi-171 were delivered. All VIP-configured 'Hip' helicopters are operated by the 4th and 15th Squadrons.

Table 25: Mil Mi-171Sh

Type	Serial no.	c/n	Delivery date	Remarks
Mi-171Sh	YI-423		15 November 2014	Assigned to 15th SOS
Mi-171Sh	YI-424		15 November 2014	Assigned to 15th SOS
Mi-171Sh	YI-425		15 November 2014	Assigned to 15th SOS
Mi-171Sh	YI-426		15 November 2014	Assigned to 15th SOS
Mi-171Sh	YI-427		15 November 2014	Assigned to 15th SOS
Mi-171Sh	YI-428		15 November 2014	Assigned to 15th SOS
Mi-171Sh	YI-429		15 November 2014	Assigned to 15th SOS
Mi-171Sh	YI-430		15 November 2014	Assigned to 15th SOS
Mi-171Sh	YI-431		13 December 2014	Assigned to 15th SOS
Mi-171Sh	YI-432		13 December 2014	Assigned to 15th SOS
Mi-171Sh	YI-433		13 December 2014	Assigned to 15th SOS
Mi-171Sh	YI-434		13 December 2014	Assigned to 15th SOS
Mi-171Sh	YI-435		2 July 2015	Assigned to 15th SOS
Mi-171Sh	YI-436		2 July 2015	Assigned to 15th SOS
Mi-171	443			Seen October 2015, probably VIP
Mi-171	YI-444			Seen October 2015, probably VIP

Note: Serial numbers are applied in black on the left side below the windscreen.

On 15 November 2014, Iraqi Army Aviation received eight Mi-171Sh aircraft including serial number YI-424. The type was assigned to the 15th SOS. (IAA pilots)

PZL-Świdnik W-3 Sokół

On 15 December 2004, Iraq signed a contract worth USD132 million with the Polish BUMAR group, covering 20 W-3 Sokół helicopters including four equipped for VIP, four configured for medical evacuation, and 12 armed assault helicopters. These were to be delivered in November 2005, and the contract also included training of 10 pilots and 24 maintenance and technical personnel. In 2005 it was planned that two units would be delivered for testing. The contract was finally cancelled in June 2006 at which point just two units were ready to be delivered.

Table 26: PZL-Świdnik W-3 Sokół

Type	Serial no.	c/n	Delivery date	Remarks
W-3A	0912	37.09.12		Cancelled
W-3A	0914	37.09.14		Cancelled

Unmanned aerial vehicles

ALIT CH-4B

In 2014, Iraq ordered CH-4B UAVs from China, probably after the visit to Iraq of the Chinese foreign minister in February of that year. The CH-4 is inspired by the General Atomics MQ-1 Predator and is designed by China Aerospace Long March International (ALIT). The CH-4B version as ordered by Iraq can carry a payload of 345kg (761lb), compared to the CH-4A that can carry a payload of 115kg (254lb). Weapons can include two HJ-10 anti-tank guided missiles, Chinese equivalents of the Lockheed Martin AGM-114 Hellfire, and two small bombs. The CH-4B has a ceiling of 23,000ft (7,010m), a cruise speed of 150-180km/h (93-112mph), a maximum speed of 210km/h (130mph), an endurance of 14 hours and an operating radius of 250km (155 miles). The first batch was received on 23 January 2015 and the first photographs (showing three vehicles) were seen in March. Thereafter, they were integrated in the apparently newly established 100th Squadron and carried out a number of reconnaissance missions from their base of al-Kut. In autumn 2015, the UAVs were attached to the 84th Attack Squadron, IAA. On 10 October, CH-4B serial number YI-801 made its first public flight during a visit to al-Kut by Iraqi Defence Minister Khaled al-Obeidi. The UAV was carrying two HJ-10s and fired one of these against a ground target southeast of Baghdad. During this mission, the UAV remained within its radio control range (250km/155 miles) and did not employ a satellite relay. A Chinese operator was present in the control room during the flight, indicating that Iraq was not yet able to employ the UAVs autonomously. Four vehicles were noted: one on the runway, one on the apron and two others in hangars.

CH-4B serial number YI-801 at al-Kut AB on the occasion of its first official flight on 10 October 2015.
(Iraqi Ministry of Defense)

Table 27: ALIT CH-4B

Type	Serial mo.	c/n	Delivery date	Remarks
CH-4B	YI-801		23 January 2015	Seen at al-Kut on 10 October 2015
CH-4B	YI-802		23 January 2015	Seen at al-Kut on 10 October 2015
CH-4B	YI-746		23 January 2015	Seen at al-Kut on 10 October 2015
CH-4B	YI-xxx		23 January 2015	Seen at al-Kut on 10 October 2015

Notes: Serial numbers are applied in black, on the both sides of the fuselage behind the wings.

A CH-4B UAV armed with two HG-10 ATGMs takes off from al-Kut AB in December 2015.
(IAA pilots)

Training aircraft

Aérospatiale SA342M Gazelle

In September 2008 Iraq began negotiations with France for the purchase of a significant quantity of Gazelle light utility helicopters. Since the last Gazelle production line (at Mostar in Bosnia and Herzegovina) had been closed for several years, France could only offer second-hand helicopters. Iraqi military interest in the Gazelle was based around plans to use the type for initial rotary-wing training. Under the supervision of the French General Directorate for Armaments, the French company Aerotec concluded a contract with Iraq to renovate and modernise six Gazelles. In 2007–08, Aerotec, based at Valence-Chabeuil airport, signed an agreement with Eurocopter and became the only French company recognised to perform overhaul of the type. The upgrade and overhaul included full inspection and repair of the airframe and engine, integration of a forward-looking infrared (FLIR) camera, a 'glass' cockpit and modern weapon systems. The company was also able to provide training for pilot instructors and technicians if necessary. By February 2010 the first four Gazelles had been prepared at Valence, and were delivered in March. The aircraft were former Aviation de Légère de l'Armée de Terre (ALAT – French Army Light Aviation) examples that had been retired from service. Technical personnel and eight IQAF instructors were trained at Bourges, France. The last two Gazelles were delivered to Iraq in May. The six helicopters were initially integrated within the 88th Attack Squadron. With the arrival of the Eurocopter EC635 in 2010, the Gazelles were handed over to the Iraqi Army Aviation College at al-Anbar. Here they are used to train pilots selected for the 55th Attack Squadron, as confirmed by Maj A:

'I joined the Army in 2007 and graduated from the Academy the following year. Then I joined the new Flight Training School that had just been created. First, I flew

On 14 June 2014 this Gazelle took off from al-Taji AB with six other helicopters to conduct raids around Samarra and in the provinces of Nineveh and Salah ad-Din.
(Iraqi Ministry of Defense)

the Cessna 172S and then switched quickly to helicopters: the Bell 206 and OH-58. I graduated as a helicopter pilot in 2010 with the Air Force College, which replaced the Training School. My first assignment was with the 88th Attack Squadron for six months training on Gazelles, on which I only flew 12 hours. My next, and current assignment was the 55th Attack Squadron on the Eurocopter EC635.'

Table 28: Aérospatiale SA342M Gazelle

Type	Serial no.	c/n	Delivery date	Remarks
SA342M	YI-295	1930	29 March 2010	ALAT in 2003, code AXL; EAALAT
SA342M	YI-296	1939		
SA342M	YI-297	1973		ALAT in 2006, code AXE; EAALAT
SA342M	YI-298	1895		ALAT in 1993; EAALAT in 2006, code AXQ
SA342M	YI-299	2008	9 June 2010	
SA342M	YI-300	1860	9 June 2010	ALAT in 1994, code AXI; EAALAT in 2004, serial AFQ; 6e Régiment d'Hélicoptères de Combat (6e RHC) serial EHR

Note: Serial numbers are applied in black on the tail, above the rotor and below an Iraqi flag. EAALAT is the Ecole d'Application de l'Aviation Légère de l'Armée de Terre – the ALAT School of Aviation.

Agusta-Bell AB206/Bell 206 JetRanger and Bell OH-58 Kiowa

The first helicopters to enter service with IAA were five former Sultan of Brunei Air Force Agusta-Bell AB206B-3 JetRangers donated by the United Arab Emirates (UAE) as early as December 2004. However, the delivery of these five Italian-built aircraft was delayed until May 2005. The helicopters arrived at Baghdad International Airport retaining their previous colours, but with UAE military roundels removed. They were initially operated by the 3rd Squadron based at New al-Muthana AB, west of Baghdad IAP, and subsequently by the 12th Training Squadron. On 3 December 2008, the Iraqi Flight Training School received five additional JetRangers from the UAE, which were transported to Iraq aboard a US Air Force Boeing C-17 Globemaster III airlifter. This next batch of JetRangers comprised examples of the US-built Bell 206B-3. These five units joined the other five Bell AB206B-3s with the 12th Training Squadron. Around the

same time, 10 former US National Guard OH-58C Kiowas were delivered to Iraq by the US Non-Standard Rotary-Wing (NSRW) office, for night flying training. They arrived at Balad AB in April 2008 and were then transferred to al-Taji and the 22nd Training Squadron. In February 2013, the 12th and 22nd Training Squadrons were renamed as the 200th and 300th Training Squadrons.

All five Bell 206B-3s, together with OH-58C Kiowa serial number 0-16223 and a Mi-171E. The helicopters were seen at Kirkuk AB on 1 March 2011 before their transfer to al-Habbaniyah AB.
(US Army)

Table 29: Agusta-Bell AB206/Bell 206 JetRanger

Type	Serial no.	c/n	Delivery date	Remarks
AB206B-3	YI-230	8683	May 2005	
AB206B-3	YI-231	8684	May 2005	
AB206B-3	YI-232	8675	May 2005	
AB206B-3	YI-233	3684	May 2005	
AB206B-3	YI-234	3683	May 2005	
206B-3	374	4374	3 December 2008	Formerly 95-04374
206B-3	395	4395	3 December 2008	Formerly 96-04395
206B-3	474	4474	3 December 2008	Formerly 98-04474
206B-3	487	4487	3 December 2008	Formerly 98-04487
206B-3	579	4579	3 December 2008	Formerly 04-04579

Note: Serial numbers are applied in black below the rotor, for the five Bell 206B-3s, and the last three digits of the construction numbers are used. For the AB206B-3, serial numbers are in the YI-23x series, but no pictures are available to confirm where these are applied.

Table 30: Bell OH-58 Kiowa

Type	Serial no.	c/n	Delivery date	Remarks
OH-58C	0-16735	40049	April 2008	Formerly 68-16735
OH-58C	0-16957	40271	April 2008	Formerly 68-16957
OH-58C	0-16148	40369	April 2008	Formerly 69-16148
OH-58C	0-16223	40444	April 2008	Formerly 69-16223
OH-58C	0-15172	40723	April 2008	Formerly 70-15172
OH-58C	0-15177	40728	April 2008	Formerly 70-15177

OH-58C	0-15300	40851	April 2008	Formerly 70-15300
OH-58C	0-15474	41025	April 2008	Formerly 70-15474
OH-58C	0-21167	41833	April 2008	Formerly 72-21167
OH-58C			April 2008	Shot down on 2 October 2013

Note: Serial numbers are applied in black below the rotor, and consist of the final six digits of the construction number.

Bell 407GX

On 1 February 2015, Iraq received 16 Bell 407GX training helicopters. This new version of the Model 407 features a new Garmin G1000 H-model 'glass' cockpit along with superior avionics and improved flight controls. These helicopters were initially delivered by Bell Helicopter to BBM Inc. of Reno, Nevada and were probably equipped to the same standard as the IA-407 (see Armed reconnaissance aircraft). The helicopters received serial numbers from YI-600 to YI-615. Once in Iraq, the aircraft were transferred to the Army Aviation College and the 200th Training Squadron.

The Iraqi Army Aviation College has 16 Bell 407GXs in service. (IAA pilots)

Table 31: Bell 407GX

Type	Serial no.	c/n	Delivery date	Remarks
Bell 407GX	YI-6XX	54505	February 2015	Formerly N512GC
Bell 407GX	YI-6XX	54506	February 2015	Formerly N512DJ
Bell 407GX	YI-6XX	54509	February 2015	Formerly N511XA
Bell 407GX	YI-6XX	54510	February 2015	Formerly N511UB
Bell 407GX	YI-6XX	54512	February 2015	Formerly N511ZA
Bell 407GX	YI-6XX	54513	February 2015	Formerly N516LS
Bell 407GX	YI-6XX	54517	February 2015	Formerly N449BH
Bell 407GX	YI-6XX	54520	February 2015	Formerly N448BH
Bell 407GX	YI-6XX	54529	February 2015	Formerly N519RH
Bell 407GX	YI-6XX	54530	February 2015	Formerly N519MD
Bell 407GX	YI-6XX	54532	February 2015	Formerly N519PP
Bell 407GX	YI-6XX	54533	February 2015	Formerly N519JW
Bell 407GX	YI-6XX	54534	February 2015	Formerly N519LA
Bell 407GX	YI-6XX	54535	February 2015	Formerly N522VC
Bell 407GX	YI-6XX	54537	February 2015	Formerly N522WF
Bell 407GX	YI-6XX	54538	February 2015	Formerly N154BW

Mil Mi-8/17

In 2012 two new squadrons were created within the Army Aviation Training School. These comprised the 16th and 85th Training Squadrons, each equipped with Mi-8 and Mi-17 helicopters formerly operated by the 4th Transport Squadron and the 15th Special Operations Squadron. Six Mi-8Ts from other sources (probably the 4th Transport Squadron) have also been transferred to the 16th Squadron.

FUTURE AIRCRAFT

Antonov An-178

On 26 August 2015 the director of the Antonov company, Mikhail Gvozdev, announced the signing of a contract for the supply of new Ukrainian military transport aircraft to Iraq. Three An-178s and one An-158 were ordered and are scheduled to be delivered by 2017. The An-178 is essentially a military version of the An-148 regional jet with a rear loading ramp (the two types share a number of components, including the forward fuselage and cockpit, and undercarriage). The An-158 is a stretched-fuselage version of the An-148, with seating for up to 99 passengers.

The An-178 tactical transport is an evolution of the An-148 airliner, powered by two Progress D-436 engines. (Vasili Koba)

Beechcraft AT-6C Texan II

On 13 May 2014 the US State Department approved the sale to Iraq of Beechcraft AT-6C Texan II light attack aircraft, including equipment, parts, training and logistical support at an estimated cost of USD790 million. The Iraqi government plans to acquire 24 AT-6Cs and equipment including two spare PT6A-68 turboprop engines, two spare AN/ALE-47 countermeasure dispensing systems and/or two spare AN/AAR-47 missile launch detection systems, non-SAASM Global Positioning Systems with CMA-4124, and aircraft parts for spares and repair.

Iraq ordered 24 AT-6Cs in 2014. These two examples each carry two GBU-12s, HMP-400 gun pods and laser-guided rockets. (Beechcraft)

Korea Aerospace Industries T-50IQ Golden Eagle

During a visit by Iraqi Prime Minister Nouri al-Maliki to South Korea in April 2011, Korea Aerospace Industries (KAI) introduced the T-50 advanced jet trainer and light combat aircraft. Three months later, negotiations began between KAI and Iraq. On 12 December 2013, Iraq placed an order for 24 T-50 training aircraft. The contract of USD2 billion included training, and follow-on support for the fleet for two decades. The first aircraft was due to be delivered in April 2016. The remaining aircraft are to be transferred within a 12-month period. Iraq will use the designation T-50IQ for its aircraft. According to sources close to the deal, the aircraft will be based on the FA-50 light combat aircraft, rather than the T-50 trainer.

On 18 July 2014, the president of KAI announced that Iraq intended to build a new airfield and repair facility in the southern part of the country in order to accommodate the 24 T-50s. The aircraft will be equipped with the UAE's Al-Tariq bomb kit, which will be integrated by a joint venture between South Africa's Denel Dynamics and Tawazun Dynamics of the UAE. Prior to training in South Korea, Iraqi pilots will study in Pakistan.

Accordingly, on 18 February 2015 the President of the Senate of Pakistan announced that his country would train Iraqi military pilots. Seven months later, it was reported

On 13 July 2015, T-50IQ serial number 5001 made its initial flight at the KAI factory airfield. (KAI)

that these pilots had begun training at the Pakistan Air Force Academy (PAFA) at Risalpur, flying K-8 Karakorum aircraft in service with the College of Flying Training.

Table 32: Korea Aerospace Industries T-50IQ Golden Eagle

Type	Serial no.	c/n	Delivery date	Remarks
T-50IQ	5001			Initial test flight at KAI factory on 13 July 2015
T-50IQ	5002			
T-50IQ	5003			
T-50IQ	5004			
T-50IQ	5005			At factory on 20 December 2015
T-50IQ	5006			At factory on 20 December 2015
T-50IQ	5007			At factory on 20 December 2015
T-50IQ	5008			At factory on 20 December 2015
T-50IQ	5009			At factory on 20 December 2015

Note: Serial numbers are applied in black on the tail. They are prefixed with 'IQAF'.

IQAF AND IAA AT WAR

The insurgency that began in Iraq shortly after the coalition invasion of 2003 initially targeted coalition armies and, latterly, Iraqi security forces when the insurgency became a sectarian civil war in February 2006. On 4 March 2008 the IAA lost its first helicopter, a Mi-17 from the 4th Transport Squadron that crashed south of Baiji due to a sandstorm, about 145km (90 miles) south of Mosul. The accident killed an American soldier and seven other people. Another Mi-17 was shot down on 27 March during heavy fighting against insurgents in northern Basra; the fate of the crew is unknown. On 28 July 2010, Mi-171 serial number YI-268 crashed near the al-Ibrahimiya Camp, 5km (3.1 miles) east of Karbala city, as the result of a sandstorm, killing the five crew-members included Col Qassem al Na'amat Mohammed, Lt Ahmed Kamel Jawad and Lt Ahmad Taleb Ali. Two other helicopters were reported lost the following year, the first on 17 May 2011 and the second on 8 August. Now, with the official withdrawal of the last US combat troops from Iraq, the responsibility for security was in the hands of the Iraqi military. On 26 July 2012, insurgents shot down an unidentified Iraqi helicopter near the town of Hadid, about 13km (8 miles) north of Baquba, the capital of Diyala province. On 19 April 2013 a helicopter (probably a Mi-17) returning from a military operation in the Tharthar area crashed near Habbaniyah AB; the four crewmembers were seriously injured. On 9 May, Mi-171 serial number 417 crash-landed during flood relief operations in southern Iraq after hitting a telecommunications tower. There were no casualties. In August 2013 three Mi-17s were deployed to Tel Abta to assist ground troops in repulsing a terrorist attack. The ground troops disembarked from the helicopters after the destruction of vehicles during an operation in the vicinity of the airport. On 2 October 2013 an OH-58 from the 300th Training Squadron was shot down during a search-and-raid operation in the Sukariya area, western Baiji district, involving several helicopters. Four crewmembers were killed in the crash, including the pilot 1st Lt Thulfiqar Jabbar, and three Iraqi Army personnel were injured during armed clashes with gunmen in the area.

Mi-171 serial number 417 crash-landed after hitting a telecommunications tower during flood relief operations in the Wasit governate on 9 May 2013.
(Arnaud Delalande Collection)

Al-Anbar campaign

IAA Mi-35Ms were first engaged as early as 22 December 2013 in the Houran valley, northeast of the province of al-Anbar, where they targeted a terrorist camp, a few weeks after their arrival in Iraq. AC-208 and King Air 350 aircraft were also used against terrorist targets in the Anbar region. In the first months of 2014, as the al-Anbar campaign against Sunni tribes began to escalate, the IAA suffered many losses, with the 4th

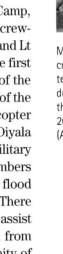

OH-58C serial number 0-16148
with 1st Lt Thulfiqar Jabbar,
who was killed on 2 October
2013 when his helicopter was
shot down during a 'search and
raid' operation in the Sukariya
area, western Baiji district.
(IAA pilots)

Transport Squadron especially hard hit. During the night of 4–5 January, Iraqi helicopters carried out air strikes on Ramadi. On the 6th, a Mi-17 crashed near Tikrit, killing its pilots Capt Mohammed Khaled Aziz and Lt Ahmed Ali Mohsen. On the 14th, helicopters intervened in Saklaouya, a city near Fallujah, against insurgents who had stormed the police station. On the 19th, Leith Yahya Al Karbalai and Sebah Abdel al-Hassan al-Gharibawi from the 2nd Utility Squadron died in the crash of their UH-1H at al-Habbaniyah AB. Two days later the IAA launched air strikes against terrorist groups in al-Anbar. On 2 February 2014, Capt Raed Hussein Ali Hussein was killed when his Mi-8 was shot down. Another Mi-17 was lost on the 22nd, in the Abu Ghraib area 25km (15miles) west of Baghdad, killing at least four crewmembers including Ahmad Al Assadi, Capt Hussein Fadhel Jasem al-Khoulalene Karma, Brig Gen Fadhil Abbas Abou Sajjad al-Tamimi and Saad al-Tai. On 8 February the IAA was engaged against gunmen who attempted to attack an Iraqi Army outpost in the north of the city of Fallujah. Between 10 and 12 February the IAA carried out 110 combat sorties in Ramadi in collaboration with IQAF King Airs. On 15 April a Mi-17 crashed west of Anbar, north of Baghdad, due to a technical problem. Three crewmembers died: Col Mohamad Arak Jasem Al Dulaimi, Lt Gen Hassan Karim Khudayr and Majid Abas Habib. On 27 April the IAA and IQAF intervened directly for the first time on Syrian territory, destroying a convoy of tanker trucks heading towards the border towards al-Anbar province.

The fall of Mosul and Tikrit

June 2014 saw Iraqi forces engaged in fierce fighting, and there were significant losses. During the battle of Mosul and the capture of the local air base by insurgents of the so-called Islamic State (IS), on 9 June, an IA-407 immobilised by a technical problem was captured. The city of Tikrit fell two days later and fighting began at the entrance to Samarra. The provinces of Ninive, Kirkuk and Salah ad-Din were now in IS hands. On 13 June a Mi-17 of the 4th Squadron was shot down in Tarmiya, north of Baghdad, and the two pilots, Capt Haydar Abdul Amir Taha Al Jaberi and Capt Ali Yasser Abdul Hussein, were killed. The next day, the IAA conducted more than 20 sorties around Samarra and in the province of Ninive and Salah ad-Din. Helicopters engaged included two Mi-171Es armed with S-8 rockets, an EC635 armed with the FN Herstal HMP-400 with 12.7mm machine gun, two IA-407s equipped with launchers for Hydra rockets, one Gazelle, and one Mi-35M (serial number YI-353) with two launchers for S-8 rockets and eight 9M120 Shturm-M/Ataka-V anti-tank missiles. Between 11 and 14 June, IS insurgents killed at least 1,500 Shia IQAF cadets in an attack on COB Speicher, officially known as Tikrit Air Academy. This mass execution became known as the Camp Speicher Massacre. Part of the camp was captured, but not the airfield. On 12 June, the pilot of a Mi-35, Capt Ahmed Mohammed Hassan, was engaged in the area of Balad city, together with the crew of an IA-407. At 12.50, the two helicopters took off from al-Taji AB and flew towards Balad city, then towards Abu Hishma city to the west of Balad AB. They identified a number of insurgents with their cars, located near a school. Two cars were destroyed in the ensuing combat. During this mission, 30 S-8 rockets, three 9K120 Ataka missiles and 160 rounds of ammunition were expended. On the 16th the same Mi-35M crashed at al-Saqlawiyah, near Fallujah, killing both pilots. The Mi-35 co-pilot in this incident was not the same as the one involved in the 12 June

mission, who went on to become one of the first pilots to train on the Mi-28. On the 20th an EC635 made an emergency landing near COB Speicher following a technical problem near Baiji. On the 26th a Mi-17 was hit by gunfire and made a hard landing at Tikrit.

On 17 July the part of COB Speicher not in IS hands, and accommodating an estimated 700 government soldiers and 150 Iranian or Iraqi Shiite militiamen, was stormed by the militants. During the night, gunmen, as well as snipers and suicide bombers, infiltrated the base and managed to reach the runway. As soon as the attack began, pilots flew aircraft out of the base to prevent their destruction, but one Russian-made helicopter that did not manage to take off was destroyed. Iraqi forces were being bombarded and mortared all night, and the next morning a number of helicopters (perhaps seven or eight) were left burning. After the fighting had stopped, some of the captured soldiers and militiamen were executed.

A rare photo shows a Mi-35M using its twin-barrel 23mm cannon during the battle of Tikrit in March 2015. It carries two S-8 rocket launchers and eight Ataka ATGM on its right stub-wing.
(Arnaud Delalande Collection)

Su-25 and Mi-28 in action

On 3 July 2014, ex-Iranian Su-25s performed several combat missions against targets in the province of Ninive. In early July, the Mi-35s were split between two bases: Balad and al-Assad. In early August, the Mi-35s were engaged in Mosul alongside the Su-25. On 8 August a Mi-171 from the 15th Special Operations Squadron crashed at Balad AB due to a technical problem. Four crewmembers were killed, including Brig Gen Hassan Alwan Al Khafaji. Four days later, a Mi-17 from the 4th Transport Squadron crashed in the Sinjar Mountains, killing five including Brig Gen Majid Abd al-Salam al-Tamimi. Around the 12th of the month, Col Jalil al-Awadi was killed after Su-25UBKM serial number 15-2458 departed the runway during a take-off from New al-Muthana AB. The aircraft was badly damaged. The day after, a Su-25 attacked vehicles on the bridge of the city of Qayyarah, 50km (31 miles) south of Mosul, in Nineveh province. The same month, Capt M. of the 35th Attack Squadron was engaged in the battle for Tikrit:

A Mi-28NE in flight over the Iraqi desert in July 2015, equipped with a rocket launcher on the left stub-wing.
(IAA pilots)

'On 2 August I personally destroyed two cannon, and others pilots one tank. On the 11th, IS attacked Jalola city in Diyala governorate. I was in Salah al-Din governorate and there were many attacks by the IQAF on IS locations in Mosul and northern Iraq. On the morning of the 12th, I was over Tikrit city along with Bell 206, Cessna 172S and Cessna 208 aircraft. Some training aircraft were used for reconnaissance missions (including the T-6). The mission was easy because IS members had started to leave the city. I was stationed at Balad AB, but my operations were not only in Salah al-Din. I also made attacks on Mosul in the fighting to recapture the dam. Between 18 and 20 August, I carried out attacks on Jorf al-Sakhir in the province of Babylon, flying from al-Assad AB. We were engaged in open fighting for Tikrit too.'

On 16 August the IAA bombarded a building in the Sadirat neighbourhood in the northern part of Tikrit, killing five insurgents. Around August/September, according to Iranian sources, a Su-25KM made an emergency landing after being hit by a MANPADS near Kirkuk. The aircraft was apparently badly damaged and removed from active service, but the pilot was unharmed. According to Iraqi pilots, at the end of August five of the 12 Su-25s were being piloted by Iraqis; the seven others were being flown by Iranian and Syrian pilots.

In early September, according to some Iraqi sources, the Mi-28 saw its first engagements just a few days after their arrival, during the fighting in al-Dhuluiya. However, this cannot be confirmed. On 11 September another Mi-17 was lost in unknown circumstances. As of mid-September, Su-25s had completed 535 combat missions. On the 16th a Mi-35M carried out three air strikes on the city of Fallujah. By 20 September, Mi-28s were in action in Jorf al-Sakhir and in the province of Salah al-Din. The next three days saw the Mi-35 lead three attacks in Fallujah and west of Ramadi. Mi-28s might also have been engaged in Baiji, south of Baghdad, in Tikrit, and in al-Anbar. On 25 September a Mi-17 was hit by 57mm cannon fire in the Salah al-Din area; the two crewmembers were wounded. In October the IAA lost two helicopters to Chinese-made FN-6 MANPADS.

Seen at New Al-Muthana AB on 7 July 2014, Su-25KM serial number 56 and Su-25UBKM serial number 58 still wear Iranian markings and each carry two FAB-250 bombs under the right wing.
(Iraqi Ministry of Defense)

On the 3rd, Mi-35 serial number YI-356 was shot down between Baiji and al-Senniyah, 210km (130 miles) north of Baghdad, killing Capt Marwan Majid Al Saadi and Capt Ziad Raad al-Khafaji. Five days later, a IA-407 was shot down in the same area while flying a support mission for a Mi-17, killing Capt Haïdar Jaber Al-Kichenassamy Salahuddin and Capt Yazan Mohammed Abdel-Rahman al-Lami. Mi-28s for their part, were now conducting operations over Anat al-Hassan in the province of Babylon. On 21 October, according to the Iraqi MoD, a Su-25SM made an emergency landing near Salah-il-Din due to a technical problem, but this time the aircraft flew again. On the 30th the Iraqi MoD announced the official engagement of the Mi-28, but by now these helicopters had certainly seen action in Baiji, south of Baghdad, in Tikrit, and al-Anbar. On 8 November Mi-35Ms were in action in Fallujah, Hit and Baiji. During the combats in Baiji, Iraqi forces captured some a number of Strela (SA-7 Grail) and FN-6 MANPADS as well as M79 Osa rockets from IS. On the 9th a Mi-35 was engaged at Amiriyat al Fallujah, 30km (19 miles) southeast of Fallujah. In mid-November, al-Assad AB became a strategic platform for Iraqi air assets engaged in combat in al-Anbar province. Six Mi-35Ms, six Mi-17s, three UH-1Hs and one Su-25 were deployed to the air base together with six US Army helicopters (two AH-64 Apaches and four UH-60 Black Hawks). On 21 November the IAA and IQAF were engaged in Ramadi and Hit, both of which were bombed.

IRIAF in combat

By the end of November 2014 the Islamic Republic of Iran Air Force (IRIAF) engaged its F-4E combat jets in support of the Peshmerga, Iraqi forces and Badr militia who launched a counterattack that aimed to retake the cities of Jalawla and Saadia in Diyala Governorate, respectively 30 and 40km (18 and 25 miles) from the Iranian border. This direct intervention was the result of a lack of operational Iraqi Su-25s. Between 20 and 23 November, three reconnaissance sorties were performed by RF-4Es. In the following days, F-4Es carried out four daily close air support (CAS) missions, employing 912

Armed with two Sattar-4 air-to-surface missiles, IRIAF F-4E Phantom II serial number 3-6682 takes off from TFB.4 Vahdati for a combat mission on 29 November 2014. (Amir Naderi)

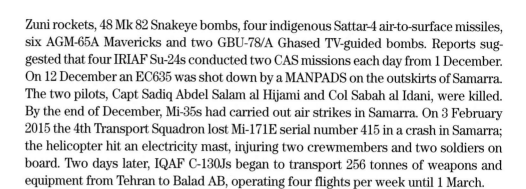
Zuni rockets, 48 Mk 82 Snakeye bombs, four indigenous Sattar-4 air-to-surface missiles, six AGM-65A Mavericks and two GBU-78/A Ghased TV-guided bombs. Reports suggested that four IRIAF Su-24s conducted two CAS missions each day from 1 December. On 12 December an EC635 was shot down by a MANPADS on the outskirts of Samarra. The two pilots, Capt Sadiq Abdel Salam al Hijami and Col Sabah al Idani, were killed. By the end of December, Mi-35s had carried out air strikes in Samarra. On 3 February 2015 the 4th Transport Squadron lost Mi-171E serial number 415 in a crash in Samarra; the helicopter hit an electricity mast, injuring two crewmembers and two soldiers on board. Two days later, IQAF C-130Js began to transport 256 tonnes of weapons and equipment from Tehran to Balad AB, operating four flights per week until 1 March.

Battle for Tikrit

On 3 March 2015 one EC635 together with two IA-407s provided CAS for the Iraqi Army in the battle to regain the oilfields of Alas and Ajeel east of Tikrit. In the following days, three Su-25s, including serial number 2513, were deployed to Balad AB. From the fleet of nine, only five examples had previously been seen combat-ready at al-Rashid AB, including serial numbers 2500, 2513, 2520 and 2522. The Su-25s carried out air support during the retaking of the highway between Tuz Khurmatu and Tikrit and the Hamrin Mountains. IAA air strikes destroyed a six-vehicle convoy on the al-'Alam-Albu Ajeel road, east of Tikrit, on 4 March. On the 5th, IS insurgents set fire to oil wells in Ajeel to hinder air strikes, but with no effect: three armoured vehicles and two explosives-laden oil tankers were hit in al-'Alam town. Iraqi Su-25s were flown by IQAF pilots, a second group of which had completed gunnery training sessions in Russia three months earlier. The Su-25s employed unguided 250kg (551lb) OFAB-250/270 bombs and S-8 rockets that lacked the precision required to hit the insurgents. Iranian Ababil-3 and Mohajer-4 UAVs were operated by IRGCASF ground control stations at al-Rashid AB and Samarra. On 10 March, IAA assets struck two car bombs and two oil tanker bombs in central Tikrit. The IAA was now using improvised bases for its helicopters. Thus, two EC635 (YI-274, YI-275) together with two IA-407s (YI-131, YI-???) and one Mi-35M (YI-361) were operating from an improvised base near Samarra. On

Su-25KM serial number 2513 at al-Rashid AB, equipped with four FAB-250 bombs, two rocket launchers and two fuel tanks, and read to take off for a bombing mission over Tikrit on 26 March 2015.
(Iraqi Ministry of Defense)

the 11th a Mi-35 decimated an eight-vehicle IS convoy escaping from Tikrit to Hawija. The same day, Iraqi forces managed to enter the Qadisiyah district. IAA again played a very important role during these operations. Three Mi-35Ms, five EC635s, five IA-407s, three UH-1Hs and six Mi-171s (from the 15th SOS) were used for attack and reconnaissance missions. Mi-35s were involved extensively for night attacks. With so many aircrafts over a small area like the city of Tikrit, the risk of 'friendly fire' put increased pressure on helicopter pilots, as remember 1st Lt M. from the 21st Attack Squadron remembers:

'An incident occurred with the commander of the 35th Squadron, during the operations to liberate Tikrit. The IA-407 of the colonel of the 21st Squadron was hit in the rotor by rounds from a Mi-35 helicopter, resulting in the destruction of two rotor blades in the upper tail, but he was able to return to Camp Speicher. The distance between the site where he was damaged and Camp Speicher was approximately 40km [25 miles]. The colonel was able to return his helicopter, semi-damaged, and with a loss of propulsion [which meant he limited to flying at low altitude]. In the same period, a pilot from the IAA learned that his home in Fallujah was in the hands of IS and had become a house for terrorists. He then asked permission to go on a mission to destroy his house, which he did by using rockets. Amazing!'

On the evening of 25 March a US-led coalition launched air strikes against IS militants in Tikrit after a request from Prime Minister Haider al-Abadi. At this time the IQAF had only five Su-25s available. The same night, 17 strike sorties were carried out by USAF F-15E Strike Eagles against central Tikrit, destroying an IS building, two bridges, three checkpoints, two staging areas, two berms, a roadblock, and a command and control facility. RAF Tornado GR.Mk 4s, supported by an Airbus Voyager tanker, used Paveway IV precision-guided bombs to attack three IS strongholds. On the 28th an F-15E conducted eight air strikes, targeting two large IS units and one IS tactical unit, and destroying one IS vehicle, one IS vehicle-borne improvised explosive device (VBIED), and 11 fighting positions. Another one fighting position was damaged. The day after, a Tornado patrol provided CAS to Iraqi forces near Tikrit, and the accuracy of the Tornado's Brimstone missile allowed a successful attack to be conducted on a

A Mi-17V-5 at the Baiji refinery airstrip on 1 March 2015. (IAA pilots)

In March 2015, during the battle of Tikrit, IAA used improvised bases to be closer to the fighting and to support operations over the city. EC635 serial number YI-275 was stationed in the Samarra area together with an IA-407. (Arnaud Delalande Collection)

A 28th Squadron pilot in the cockpit of a Mi-28NE shortly after take-off from al-Taji AB in May 2015.
(IAA pilots)

terrorist armoured personnel carrier positioned under a road bridge. At the beginning of April, Mi-35s carried out air strikes near al-Huija in the south of Kirkuk. By 2 April, Iraqi forces had full control of the city of Tikrit and had begun to redeploy its regular and special forces towards Baiji and its refinery, which was seized in early March. On 13 March, RAF Tornados provided CAS for Iraqi ground forces in and around Baiji, attacking four buildings within an IS military compound with Paveway IVs. During the night of the 18th an IQAF C-130J dropped 10 tons of supplies for Iraqi forces engaged in the battle of Baiji. The day after, two Su-25s took off from Balad AB and provided CAS around the city, each armed with two B-8M1 rocket pods. By 25 March at the latest, Iraqi Mi-28s (now with N025E radar) were engaged in combat from al-Taji, operating to the north of Baghdad together with one IA-407, one Mi-35, one UH-1H, two Mi-171Sh, one Mi-171E from the 15th SOS and one EC635. Between them they carried out a rescue mission near Therthar Dam, saving 13 soldiers of the Iraqi Army's 4th Regiment, 1st Division, who were trapped by IS militants after their headquarters had been besieged. Maj A. was not directly engaged in the battles for Tikrit and Baiji, but remembers this intense period:

'My missions in the 55th Attack Squadron are reconnaissance, support for ground forces, VIP escort, fast ground attacks and cover for Mi-17s involved in rescues. I was not engaged in the battle of Tikrit in March, only later. At that time, I was in Anbar province to protect al-Assad AB and support ground forces in al-Baghdady and Haditha. Helicopters were often hit by ground fire. Personally, I was hit seven times, most of them by 12.7mm. One of the shots was made by a sniper, very close to my face, and hit the door next to me. The injuries to my face were minor. Another time, during one of my missions, I had to land at al-Karmah, next to IS forces, after my helicopter was shot at. I lost one of my four blades, then I flew back with the same helicopter to al-Taji, but I lost lift, max torque, high descent and low speed. My co-pilot and I ran and IS didn't catch us. In that mission, I figured out that I should not fight with IS with too many emotions. Think, don't fight if you want to stay alive. It's a long story as to how IS ran after me, but I make it short. I landed at 11.00 and I came back to the air base at about 17.00.'

The last incident recounted by Maj A. could have taken place on 22 April, when an EC635 was hit by enemy fire and was written off. On 17 May, Ramadi fell into IS hands, after they took advantage of a sandstorm to attack, Iraqi and US warplanes and helicopters not being able to take off to launch air strikes. On the 19th two Mi-17s protected by an IA-407 made a rescue flight into Ramadi to evacuate 28 officers and soldiers trapped by IS. The troops were airlifted from a location in the district of al-Mallab. These rescue missions exposed pilots to the small arms fire, as 21st Attack Squadron pilot 1st Lt M. recalls:

'During an escort mission, my helicopter was hit by AK-47 – a big hole in the windscreen. Thanks to God, I was not injured.'

On 24 May a Su-25 destroyed a very large ammunition dump and four buildings in Ramadi. Two days after, a helicopter operation was mounted to rescue two injured soldiers in the area of al-Kasarat, located 80km (50 miles) south of Tikrit.

Beginning in June, air strikes targeted numerous IS convoys in the al-Qa'im district of al-Anbar province, as well as a large complex that assembled car bombs and IEDs in Kirkuk's Hawija district. On the 17th, IAA attack helicopters carried out aerial bombardment of the IS camp known as Camp al-Zarqawi, in the area of Zawiyah, Hit district, killing many fighters including two IS leaders. On the 25th, four fuel tankers loaded with fuel and three vehicles loaded with arms and ammunition were destroyed by helicopters to the south of the area of Siniya, west of Beiji district. On 6 July, while on final approach to al-Rashid AB, a Su-25 released a bomb over a residential area in the west of Baghdad, as the result of a technical malfunction. Three houses were destroyed and 12 people killed. The same day, IAA together with the al-Furat al-Awsat Operations Command conducted an airborne operation in the Onak al-Raza area, deep within al-Anbar province. The landing operation targeted a gathering of IS militants and resulted in the destruction of the group and its vehicles as well as 40 boats that had been prepared to carry out an operation in al-Habbaniyah. On 13 July an EC635 crash-landed in Kermah, near Fallujah, due to shrapnel damage (either from its own ordnance or enemy fire). The helicopter caught fire during its descent, but the crew was unharmed. On the 29th the IAA, using accurate intelligence, destroyed the headquarters of the so-called Diwan al-Hesba in al-Ratba, western Anbar, killing 13 militants, including senior IS leaders. Beginning in August, Iraqi Su-25s destroyed 16 IS oil tanker trucks, which were smuggling oil out of the oilfields in Qayyarah, south of Mosul. On the 6th, Iraqi aircraft carried out precision strikes against terrorist hideouts in the city of Husaybah, 7km (4 miles) east of Ramadi, as well as in al-Malahmeh and Albu Alwan, destroying nine arms depots, 22 armoured vehicles and 14 cars. On the 13th the IAA, again exploiting accurate intelligence, managed to destroy two shelters belonging to IS militants and two workshops for booby-trapping vehicles in Fallujah, as well as an IS communications centre for the district. On the 22nd, Mi-35M serial number YI-161 made an emergency landing in a safe area west of Samarra after hitting a power line. The crew was injured and the helicopter suffered damage after catching fire. A technical team examined the damage before transferring the helicopter to base where it was eventually repaired and apparently returned to service. However, photographs show the helicopter suffered structural damage, especially to the tail, part of which was missing. Four days later, the IQAF carried out two sorties based on intelligence from the Intelligence and Investigations Agency. The first strike targeted an IS convoy in Anbar near the Syrian-Iraqi border, while the second strike targeted a con-

F-16IQ serial number 1604 at Balad AB on 6 September 2015, four days after the launch of combat operations in the Salah ad-Din and Kirkuk provinces. (Iraqi Ministry of Defense)

voy in the al-Wailiya area in Anbar. Numerous IS militants were killed during these two raids, including two IS leaders. On the 30th, reports indicated that US Apache attack helicopters had arrived at al-Habbaniyah AB, east of Ramadi. The same day, an IQAF air raid in al-Qa'im reportedly destroyed the IS cell responsible for the recent killings of two Iraqi generals. On the 31st, air strikes in Ba'aj killed three IS commanders. On 2 September the IQAF bombarded a convoy in Kasiriyat, Haditha.

F-16 goes to war

On 6 September 2015 the Iraqi MoD announced that the F-16IQ had begun combat operations four days previously. The fighters carried out a reconnaissance mission and 15 air strikes on enemy positions in the Salah ad-Din and Kirkuk provinces, north of Baghdad. On the 5th, targets were an explosives manufacturing laboratory and a house where a meeting of IS leaders was taking place in Hawija, 40km (25 miles) northwest of Baiji. Iraqi F-16s also bombed a convoy belonging to the organisation that was heading from Sinjar to Tal Afar, south of Mosul, killing seven IS members and wounding 12 others, as well as destroying three vehicles. Three aircraft were engaged 19 minutes after the receipt of the information from intelligence. On the 12th, IAA helicopters destroyed two armoured bulldozers used by IS to open up defences near Siniya in the Baiji area. On the 14th, F-16s of the IQAF carried out several strikes targeting IS locations near Hawija, (55km/34 miles west of the city of Kirkuk) and also resulting in the complete destruction of the bridge on the Zab River, 95km (59 miles) west of Kirkuk. This bridge had been used to transfer IS militants and supplies from the Syrian city of Raqqa, via Mosul, to Sharqat parties of Baiji and Hawijah to access to areas south and west of Kirkuk. On the 24th, F-16s conducted air strikes in Mosul, hitting IED factories and car bomb workshops.

On 28 September, IA-407 serial number YI-125 crashed-land west of COB Speicher, coming down in a desert area north of Tikrit. An EC635 that accompanied it was able to rescue the two crewmembers. According to local witnesses, the helicopter was hit by ground fire, but the Iraqi MoD denied this and attributed the crash to a technical problem. On 5 October, Iraqi F-16s conducted an air strike on a house in Qaim, Anbar province, used as a hideout for IS militants and as a warehouse for explosives, resulting in the destruction of the house, as well as the killing of 20 terrorists. On the 13th, Su-25s flew an air strike against a convoy of IS vehicles heading towards the city of Fallujah. The bombing killed 25 militants, injuring 30 others and destroying nine vehicles. Another strike launched in the Albu Shejel area in Khalidiya Island, a city located northwest of Fallujah, killed 12 IS militants and wounded 10 others. The same day, Mi-35Ms using Ataka missiles destroyed four truck bombs that were heading towards Iraqi positions in Seneia town, west of Baiji. On the 15th, another convoy, this time heading to Mosul, was hit by Iraqi F-16s near the town of al-Shirqat, 50km (31 miles) north of Baiji, together with three IS hideouts. With the introduction of the F-16, IQAF air strikes became more intense and attacks more accurate. On the 17th the new fighters destroyed two targets in two different locations: an arms depot in Albu Shajil, northern Fallujah, and a cave in Mount Makhoul where IS militants were barricaded, together with materiel amassed on the side of the road in the village of Almsalkhh Aelloukah. The same day, Mi-28s were engaged in the Albu Faraj area, near

F-16 serial number 1611 is seen in August 2015, while still assigned to the 162nd FW in Tuscon, but with an external load that includes AIM-9L/M Sidewinder air-to-air missiles, a Sniper targeting pod and multiple ejector racks for free-fall bombs.
(Stephan de Bruijn)

Ramadi. Numerous IS positions were destroyed using Ataka missiles and rockets. On the 18th the IQAF attacked an IS convoy while supporting the Iraqi Security Forces and al-Hashed al-Shaabi militia fighting in the al-Fatha area in the north of Salah ad-Din province. In the process they killed 20 IS fighters and destroyed seven vehicles carrying weapons.

On 25 September an Iraqi F-16 used intelligence information to target an IS headquarters in the district of Kabisa, 70km (44 miles) west of Ramadi, killing nine militants and destroying two fuel tanks and two vehicles. Between 2 September and 31 October, F-16s carried out 62 sorties (including 12 in Mosul, 14 in Anbar and six in Salah al-Din provinces) and destroyed 160 targets. Since the beginning of their engagement in June 2014, Su-25s had dropped more than 3,900 'dumb' bombs, fired 15,536 rounds of 30mm ammunition and 10,269 S-8 rockets. C-130J and An-32 transport aircraft had transferred 442,809 fighters and 18,312 tonnes of cargo, and Cessna 208s had fired nearly 1,770 Hellfire missiles.

On 2 November, US aircraft landed at al-Assad AB with special military reinforcements, which resulted in the closure of the base for three days. Two days later, a Mi-35M was hit by ground fire west of Ramadi. One of the rounds penetrated the cabin and hit the pilot, Capt Maher Hasan who managed to continue flying and perform an emergency landing in a safe area despite being injured. On the 12th, Iraqi warplanes bombed vehicles at Albu Shajel in Khalidiya Island (23km/14 miles east of Ramadi).

In November a number of Mi-171Es from the 4th Transport Squadron, including serial number 414, were transferred in Erbil to provide medical evacuation service. On the 13th they carried out support for forces in the Sinjar operation, transporting wounded Peshmerga. Three days later, IS elements launched an offensive against Iraqi forces' position in the Mount Makhoul area, north of Baiji. The IAA, including EC635s, together with IQAF Cessna 208s of the 3rd Attack and Reconnaissance Squadron and Su-25s of the 109th Attack Squadron, took part in repelling the attack.

First UAV engagement

On 6 December 2015 a CH-4B from the 84th Attack Squadron was engaged for the first time during an air strike in Ramadi, destroying an artillery piece hidden in a factory. This gun was targeting Iraqi forces stationed at Palestine Bridge, northwest of the city.

This bridge, which crosses the Euphrates River, was regained by Iraqi Security Forces (ISF) and Iraqi Counter-terrorism Forces (ICT) on 25 November, with the support of bombing by the international coalition. This cut Islamic State's last supply line into the western city of Ramadi. The day after, Iraqi Su-25s destroyed two labs used for booby-trapping vehicles and the manufacture of IEDs in an air strike west of Samarra. Another air raid resulted in the destruction of four booby-trapping vehicles in Samarra Island. A few days after, one of the Iraqi UAVs targeted a gathering of IS fighters, to the west of the city of Ramadi, destroying one vehicle with an HG-10 missile. On 4 and 5 December, militants employed several car bombs against the positions of government forces. At least six car bombs were destroyed, and eight others intercepted.

On 9 December a CH-4B destroyed an explosives manufacturing plant in the area of al-Kiara. On 16 February 2016, another UAV destroyed an equipment depot. The same day, the 85th Training Squadron lost one of its Mi-17s in the eastern part of al-Kut city. The helicopter was on the way from Shuaiba AB to al-Taji AB when it suffered a technical problem, killing nine soldiers including the two pilots, Capts Mohammed Qasim and Mohammed Ghaeb. The day after, an IA-407 from the 21st Armed Reconnaissance Squadron was shot down near Amiriyat al-Fallujah. The two crewmembers, Maj Ahmed Nehru and 1st Lt Oumid, were killed. On 1 March operations began with the aim of liberating Samarra Island with the support of Mi-35Ms (including serial number YI-366). An IS HQ located on a farm near Samarra was bombed by Su-25s while CH-4Bs neutralised VBIEDs west of Samarra.

On 16 March 2016, Cessna AC-208B serial number YI-119 crashed in the vicinity of Hawjah, near Kirkuk. According to IS militants, the aircraft was shot down by a 57mm anti-aircraft gun. The three crewmembers (Brig Gen Ali Falih, Col Mohammed Kazem and Maj Mohamed Abdel Wahab) were killed.

A CH-4B UAV armed with four HG-10 ATGMs ready to take off from al-Kut AB during one of its first engagements in December 2015.
(IAA pilots)

APPENDIX I: ORDERS OF BATTLE

Iraqi Air Force Order of Battle

Ali Air Base

3rd Squadron
TC-208

70th Reconnaissance Squadron
CH-2000, SB7L-360

Flying Training Wing

201st Training Squadron
Cessna 172S

202nd Training Squadron
Lasta-95N

203rd Training Squadron
T-6A

al-Rashid Air Base

109th Attack Squadron
Su-25

Balad Air Base

3rd Attack and Reconnaissance Squadron
AC-208, RC-208

9th Fighter Squadron
F-16C/D

115th Squadron
L-159

New al-Muthana Air Base

23rd Transport Squadron
C-130E/J

33rd Transport Squadron
An-32B

62nd Utility Squadron
U-28

87th Reconnaissance Squadron
King Air 350ER/ISR, 350ER/LTA

?? Transport Squadron
DHC-6

Iraqi Army Aviation Order of Battle

al-Habbaniyah Air Base

Army Aviation College

16th Training Squadron
Mi-8T, Mi-17V-5, Mi-17E (CT)

85th Training Squadron
Mi-17V-5, Mi-17E (CT)

88th Attack Squadron
SA342M

200th Training Squadron
AB206B-3, Bell 206B-3, Bell 407GX

300th Training Squadron
OH-58C

al-Kut Air Base

2nd Utillity Squadron
UH-1H

4th Transport Squadron
Mi-171E

15th Special Operations Squadron
Mi-171Sh

21st Armed Reconnaissance Squadron
Bell IA-407, 407T

28th Attack Squadron
Mi-28NE

35th Attack Squadron
Mi-35M

55th Attack Squadron
EC635T2+, EC135P2+

84th Squadron
CH-4

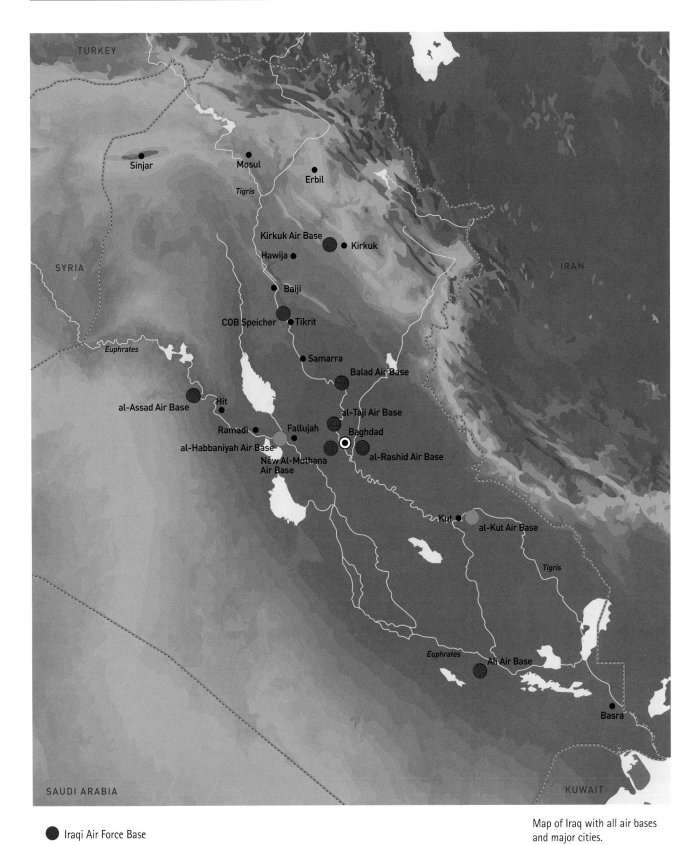

● Iraqi Air Force Base

● Iraqi Army Aviation Base

Map of Iraq with all air bases
and major cities.
(Map by James Lawrence)

APPENDIX II:
ATTRITION

Table 33: Confirmed IQAF and IAA attrition, 2005–16

Date	Unit	Aircraft	Serial no. and c/n	Remarks
30 May 2005	3rd Squadron, IQAF	7SLX		Crashed near Jalula, about 80km (50 miles) northeast of Baquba, during operational mission from Kirkuk AB; four US servicemen and one Iraqi airman KIA
4 March 2008	4th Squadron, IAA	Mi-17V-5		Crashed south of Baiji due to sandstorm; Lt Jassim Mohammed Dagher, 1st Lt Barac Jihad + 6 KIA including one US soldier
27 March 2008	4th Squadron, IAA	Mi-17V-5		Shot down northern Basra
28 July 2010	IAA	Mi-17V-5	YI-268	Crashed near Karbala; Col Qassem al Na'amat Mohammed, Lt Ali Fadel Ibrahim + 1 KIA
17 May 2011	IAA	Mi-17?		Col Yassin Ibrahim Khudair KIA
8 August 2011	IAA	Mi-17?		
26 July 2012	IAA	Mi-17?		Shot down near town of Hadid, about 13km (8 miles) north of Baquba, Diyala province; fate of crew unknown
19 April 2013	IAA	Mi-17?		Crashed near al-Habbaniya AB; four crew seriously injured
9 May 2013	15th Squadron, IAA	Mi-171E	417	Crash-landed in Wasit during flood relief operations; crew safe
2 October 2013	300th Squadron, IAA	OH-58C		Shot down near Baiji; 1st Lt Thulfiqar Jabbar, Col Yassin Mahmoud Salem + 2 KIA
6 January 2014	2nd Squadron, IAA	UH-1H		Crashed near Tikrit; Capt Mohammed Khalid Aziz, Lt Ahmed Ali Mohsen KIA
19 January 2014	4th Squadron, IAA	Mi-17		Crashed al-Habbaniya AB due to technical problem; Leith Yahya Al Karbalai, Sebah Abdel al-Hassan al-Gharibawi + 2 KIA
2 February 2014	4th Squadron, IAA	Mi-8		Shot down; Maj Hussein Ali Hussein KIA
22 February 2014	4th Squadron, IAA	Mi-17		Shot down in Abu Ghraib area 25km (16 miles) west of Baghdad; Capt Jassim Hussein Saud, Brig Gen Fadel Abbas Mohsen + 4 KIA
15 April 2014	4th Squadron, IAA	Mi-17		Crashed west of Anbar, north of Baghdad due to technical problem; Maj Jassim Mohammed Fray, Lt Gen Hassan Karim Khudayr, Brig Ammar Abdul Abbas Habibi KIA
9 June 2014	21st Squadron, IAA	IA-407		Captured al-Mosul when taking the base
13 June 2014	4th Squadron, IAA	Mi-17		Shot down at Tarmiya, north of Baghdad; Capt. Haydar Abdul Amir Taha Al Jaberi, Capt. Ali Yasser Abdul Hussein KIA
16 June 2014	35th Squadron, IAA	Mi-35M	YI-352	Crashed al-Saqlawiyah near Fallujah; Capt Ahmed Mohammed Hassan, Capt Mustafa Ismail Khalil Tayeh Al Kaabi + 1 KIA
20 June 2014	55th Squadron, IAA	EC635		Emergency landing COB Speicher due to technical problem near Baiji; crew safe

17 July 2014	IAA	Mi-??		Destroyed on ground at COB Speicher
18 July 2014	IAA	7 to 8 unidentified helicopters		Destroyed on ground at COB Speicher by IS mortar bombardment
8 August 2014	15th Squadron, IAA	Mi-171E		Crashed Balad AB due to technical problem; Capt Hadi Sadiq Morteza, Brig Gen Alaa Hassan Alwan Al Tayer + 3 KIA
August 2014	109th Squadron, IQAF	Su-25UBKM		Crashed after runway overrun during take-off at New al-Muthana AB; Col Jalil Hamid al-Awadi KIA
12 August 2014	4th Squadron, IAA	Mi-171E		Crashed in Sinjar Mountains; Brig Gen Majed Abdul Salam Salem + 1 KIA
11 September 2014	IAA	Mi-17?		Col Abdul Sattar Abdul Hadi al-Bashir KIA
September 2014	109th Squadron, IQAF	Su-25SM		Emergency landing after being hit by MANPADS near Kirkuk, aircraft removed from active service; pilot safe
25 September 2014	IAA	Mi-17		Damaged by 57mm anti-aircraft fire in Salah al-Din area; Lt Col Hussein Ali Abdullah KIA, one crew WIA
3 October 2014	35th Squadron, IAA	Mi-35M	YI-356	Shot down by FN-6 MANPADS between Baiji and al-Senniyah, 210km (130 miles) north of Baghdad; Capt Marwan Majid Abbas, Maj Ziad Raad KIA
8 October 2014	21st Squadron, IAA	IA-407		Shot down by FN-6 MANPADS near Baiji during support mission for a Mi-17; Capt Haidar Hamad Jaber, Capt Yazan Mohammed Abdel-Rahman al-Lami KIA
21 October 2014	109th Squadron, IQAF	Su-25		Emergency landing due to technical problem near Salah ad-Din; pilot safe
12 December 2014	55th Squadron, IAA	EC635		Shot down by MANPADS on outskirts of Samarra; Capt Sadiq Abdel Salam al Hijami, Col Sabah Abbas al Idani KIA
3 February 2015	4th Squadron, IAA	Mi-171E	415	Crashed Samarra; two crew WIA
6 March 2015	No. 4 Squadron, RJAF	T67 Firefly		Crashed during training; Jordanian instructor Col Mamdouh al-Amiri, student Lt Laith Ali Nasser KIA
22 April 2015	55th Squadron, IAA	EC635		Hit by enemy fire; written off
25 June 2015	9th Squadron, IQAF/162nd FW	F-16C	1609	Crashed 8km (5 miles) east of Douglas Municipal Airport, US; Brig Gen Rafid Mohammad Hassan KIA
13 July 2015	55th Squadron, IAA	EC635		Crash-landed near Kermah, near Fallujah; crew safe
22 August 2015	35th Squadron, IAA	Mi-35M	YI-161	Crash-landed west of Samarra after hitting power line. Crew injured
28 September 2015	21st Squadron, IAA	IA-407	YI-125	Hit by ground fire and crash-landed west of COB Speicher; crew rescued by EC635
4 November 2015	35th Squadron, IAA	Mi-35M		Emergency landing after being hit by ground fire west of Ramadi; Capt Maher Hasan injured
16 February 2016	85th Squadron, IAA	Mi-17		Crashed eastern al-Kut city after suffering technical problem; Capt Mohammed Qasim, Capt Mohammed Ghaeb + 7 KIA
17 February 2016	21st Squadron, IAA	IA-407		Shot down near Amiriyat Al-Fallujah; Maj Ahmed Nehru, 1st Lt Oumid KIA
16 March 2016	3rd Squadron, IQAF	AC-208B	YI-119	Shot down in the vicinity of Hawjah, near Kirkuk, reportedly by anti-aircraft fire; Brig Gen Ali Falih, Col Mohammed Kazem, Maj Mohamed Abdel Wahab KIA

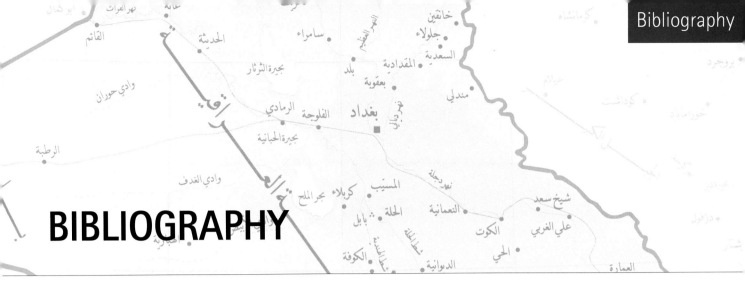

BIBLIOGRAPHY

BAUER, M., *Training the Iraqi Air Force – Lessons from a U.S. C-130 Advisory Mission*, (Washington Institute for Near East Policy, August 2007)

COOPER, T., AND SADIK, Brig Gen A., *Iraqi Fighters: 1953–2003: Camouflage & Markings*, (Harpia Publishing, L.L.C., June 2008) ISBN 978-0615214146

DELALANDE, A., 'Iraqi Air Power Reborn', *Combat Aircraft Monthly*, Vol. 16 No. 4, April 2015

DIJKSHOORN, M., *Scramble, Iraq Order of Battle*, (www.scramble.nl/orbats/iraq/overview)

ELLIOT, D. J., *Long War Journal*, various articles, (www.longwarjournal.org/archives/author/enemy)

ELLIOT, D. J., *Montrose Toast – Iraq Order of Battle*, (home.comcast.net/~djyae/site/?/page/Iraq_Order_of_Battle)

FROST, C., 'Iraqi Flight Training School takes off', *The Advisor*, 15 March 2008

Kampfly, *Iraq – the new Air Force* (www.kampfly.dk/Flysiden/Lande/Asien/Irak.htm)

RIPLEY, T., *Middle East Air Power in the 21st Century*, (Pen & Sword Aviation, February 2010) ISBN 978-1848840997

SMITH, S., *Deployed Flight Test of the Iraqi Air Force Comp Air 7SLX*, (Air Force Test Center History Office, February 2014)

TAGHVAEE, B., 'Iran takes on Islamic State', *Combat Aircraft Monthly*, Vol. 16 No. 2, February 2015

TAGHVAEE, B., 'Air war over Tikrit', *Combat Aircraft Monthly*, Vol. 16 No. 6, June 2015

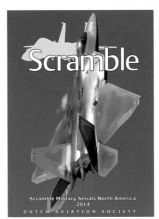

HARPIA PUBLISHING+

Glide With Us Into The World of Aviation Literature

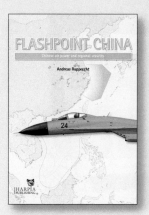

Flashpoint China: Chinese air power and regional security

Andreas Rupprecht

80 pages, 28 x 21 cm, softcover

18.95 Euro, ISBN 978-0-9854554-8-4

From the South China Sea to the mountains of Nepal, the continued economic rise of the People's Republic of China has led to a dramatic shift in the balance of power in the region. As a result, the relationship between China and its neighbours, as well as with the United States and its allies, has become increasingly important for the future of the region – and for the rest of the world.

One of the first books in an all-new format from Harpia Publishing, this uniquely compact yet comprehensive work provides a richly illustrated, in-depth analysis and overview of the most important conflicts in which China is currently involved – and those that it is likely to be involved with in the future – with a particular focus on regional air power and respective balances of strength.

Russia's Warplanes Volume 1: Russian-made Military Aircraft and Helicopters Today

Piotr Butowski

256 pages, 28 x 21 cm, softcover

35.95 Euro, ISBN 978-0-9854554-5-3

Written by an acknowledged expert in the field, *Russia's Warplanes* is as an exhaustive directory of the latest products of Russia's military aviation industry. As well as outlining aircraft that currently equip the various Russian air arms, the first of two volumes also takes into account aircraft developed for and fielded by foreign states in the post-Soviet era.

Piotr Butowski provides authoritative technical descriptions for each military aircraft – and every significant sub-variant – currently available from Russia's aerospace industry, or otherwise in large-scale service. With the level of accuracy and insight familiar to Harpia's regular readers, each aircraft profile also includes specifications, and details of operators, upgrades, avionics and weapons.

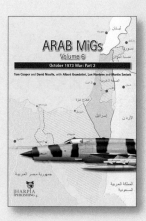

Arab MiGs Volume 6 | October 1973 War: Part 2

Tom Cooper and David Nicolle, with Albert Grandolini, Lon Nordeen and Martin Smisek

256 pages, 28 x 21 cm, softcover

35.95 Euro, ISBN 978-0-9854554-6-0

Continuing Harpia Publishing's renowned coverage of air actions by Arab air forces during the October 1973 Arab-Israeli War, the sixth volume in this series sees the authors continue their research in the Middle East, interviewing and discussing the fighting in detail with pilots, participants and eyewitnesses from almost every unit involved. The result is the first-ever coherent narrative of this air war. Supported by a plethora of background information, more than 300 photographs, colour profiles, maps and diagrams depicting the action, aircraft, camouflage patterns, markings, and weaponry deployed, *Arab MiGs Volume 6* is set to become a standard reference work on the subject.

THE AVIATION BOOKS OF A DIFFERENT KIND

UNIQUE TOPICS I **IN-DEPTH RESEARCH** I **RARE PICTURES** I **HIGH PRINTING QUALITY**

www.harpia-publishing.com